Temple Lore

A Historical Study of Temples and Invasions in South India

Temple Lore

A Historical Study of Temples and Invasions in South India

Dr R Srinivasan

an imprint of Highlyy Publishing LLP

*Dedicated to my parents
Shri. V. Rajamanickam &
Srimati. Kalavathi Rajamanickam
and all the children of the family*

ISBN: 978-93-6009-118-7 (Hardback)
First Published : 2024
Copyright ©Author

Publisher's Note:

All Rights reserved under International Copyright Conventions. No part of this publication may be reproduced, stored in a retrieval system, or transmitted in any form or by any means, electronic, mechanical, photocopying, recording or otherwise without the prior written consent of the publisher and the copyright owner.

The content of this book is the sole expression and opinion of its author(s), and not of the publisher. The publisher in no manner is liable for any opinion or views expressed by the author(s). While best efforts have been made in preparing the book, the publisher makes no representations or warranties of any kind and assumes no liabilities of any kind with respect to the accuracy or completeness of the content and specifically disclaims any implied warranties of merchantability or fitness of use of a particular purpose.

The publisher believes that the contents of this book do not violate any existing copyright/intellectual property of others in any manner whatsoever. However, in case any source has not been duly attributed; the publisher may be notified in writing for necessary action.

> Cataloging in Publication Data--DK
>
> Courtesy: D.K. Agencies (P) Ltd. <docinfo@dkagencies.com>
>
> Srinivasan, R., 1961- author.
>
> Temple lore : a historical study of temples and invasions in South India / Dr R Srinivasan.
>
> pages cm
>
> Includes texts in Sanskrit (Devanagari and roman).
>
> Includes bibliographical references.
>
> ISBN 9789360091187 (hardback)
>
> 1. Hindu temples--India, South--History. 2. Folklore--India, South. 3. India, South--Religious life and customs. 4. India, South--History.   I. Title.
>
> LCC BL1243.76.S68S65 2024 | DDC 294.53509548   23

Published by :

Correspondence
Address :

an imprint of Highlyy Publishing LLP
4/30 A II Floor, Double Storey Buildings
Vijay Nagar, Delhi-110009
Editorial: +91 9811026449
Sales : +91 9999953412
Email: info@howacademics.com
Website: www.howacademics.com

Contents

Acknowledgement   *ix*
Preface   *xi*
Introduction   *xiii*
Historical Context   *xxvii*

1.	Vellayi and the Story of Sri Rangam	1
2.	Pin Thodarntha Valli	5
3.	Tulukka Nachiar	9
4.	The Story of Namperumal	13
5.	Ramanuja and Bibi Nachiar	21
6.	Malik Kafur and the Looting of Madurai	33
7.	Tipu, Marathas and Sringeri Matha	39
8.	Vidyaranya and the Making of Vijayanagara Empire	45
9.	The Story of Alipiri (Tirumala)	51
10.	Sultan Tanah Shah and Ramadasu	55
11.	The In-Laws of Lord Venkateshwara Swamy	69
12.	A Temple for Duryodhana	73
13.	Robert Clive's Makarakandi	79
14.	William Garrow: A Matter of Faith	85
15.	Sir Thomas Munro and the Story of Mantralaya	89

Epilogue   *93*
Index   *95*

Acknowledgement

This book is inspired by the stories related to temples of South India narrated by my parents and other relatives throughout my childhood. I am indebted to them for their brilliant narrations that made me curious to learn more.

My wife, Chitra Srinivasan, worked with me, proof read and provided valuable inputs. She also added from the reservoir of her own expertise on matters related to such narratives. This book is actually a mark of my gratitude to her for her invaluable support in this delightful endeavor.

My sons, Deepak Sharma and Dr. Sashank Srinivasan have been ardent listeners to these stories right from their childhood. Their curiosity and insightful questions prompted me to explore these stories from historical perspective. Hopefully, the versions fortified with historical evidences now would continue to be narrated to the children of our family and to those of the readers.

In all such endeavors, friends do play an important role. In my case, Dr. Anurada Dinesh, a longtime friend and my ardent critic in absolute positive sense, has prompted me to undertake this exploration and give them a shape in the form of this book.

I owe my gratitude to the named and unnamed authors of numerous blogs and websites that provided exhilarating versions of the stories concerned. Without such substantial variations in their versions, my own curiosity would have remained unprovoked. I have endeavored to cite them, wherever their versions were necessary for discussion.

The images that are incorporated in the book are from open sources with appropriate mention. Even images obtained from Wiki pedia carry the names of the original owners, to the extent that I could find them. I owe all these sources immense gratitude.

I am grateful to Lord Ranganatha for sustaining my curiosity and showing me the directions for discovering important historical insights that have enriched me further and endowed me with insatiable curiosity to understand and explore the rich cultural heritage of South India.

R Srinivasan

Preface

In the early years of every child in the world, especially in India and South India, grandparents and parents narrating stories from epics and remembered history is a prevalent practice. Many a times, angels and demons, heroes and villains of such stories foster greater curiosity in children to explore the rich mosaic of cultural tapestry, heritage and history of the land that they grow up in.

I grew up in traditional Tamil Nadu. Though I was born in 1961 in a fairly big town, my early years and primary schooling were in villages where agraharam[1] existed, village life was filed with excitements of temple chariot festivals and bull fights. People had a story to narrate for everything that happened or did not happen. Even a thunder storm, a failure of monsoons or abundance of harvest had stories of kings or saints or demons attached to them. I vividly recall my great grandmother urging us to close our eyes and ardently call out 'Arjuna, Arjuna' so that no lightening will strike us during thunder storms! Curiously, very life itself revolved around gods, stories of devotees and demons that are immortal in Indian culture.

My father and mother had grown up in orthodox households that were surprisingly more liberal in their outlook, albeit with deep religious and spiritual roots. I had the good fortune to be with my grandparents too who were repositories of knowledge and history of their times. This was amply supplemented by my uncles and aunts who had their own stock of stories to narrate from every epic and purana. In short, I grew up with these stories that parched my throat, palpitated my heart and became the theme of dreams in my childhood.

These stories that I had heard kept prompting me to study relevant sources, thereby initiating me into the wondrous world of studies in history. Though I graduated in Physics and took up masters in Social Work and a PhD in Political Sociology, history and culture continue to hold predominant interest. As time passed by, I collected many such stories, passing them on to my own children

---

1 Agraharam refers to streets that surround the village temple where Brahmin priests attached to the temples reside. Over many recent decades, these agraharams have disappeared owing to social mobilization and migration.

whose starry eyed audience prompted me to explore the historical background of many such stories.

This book of fifteen stories concerning some of the temples in South India is a product of this curiosity to discover the events in history concerning them. I have delved into historical records, archival material and books by acclaimed historians like KA Nilakanta Sastri, Robert Sewell, AL Basham, etc., to trace the dots in history that connect these stories to physical occurrences. They present either evidence to support them or otherwise, without in any manner questioning their cultural or religious significance.

No claim can be made as to the apodictic support or denial of each story since the scholastic standards that we apply to research cannot be adopted to oral traditions with equal vigor. This is further constrained by my own limitation as a historian and my ability to reach out to more substantial sources. In any case, this endeavor was prompted to gain a larger understanding of events that created these stories with no intention to avow or disavow their cultural significance. However, one claim can certainly be made: This exploration by itself has given me an opportunity to understand the history of South India (and history of India in general) in much more substantial detail.

I do hope that readers of this book will also gain similar advantage and their curiosity will lead to discovery of more insights based on historical evidence, enriching the cultural heritage of our great nation and South India in due course of time.

Dr. R Srinivasan

Introduction

Oral traditions and histories are vital to all civilizations. They lend a vibrancy to culture, sustaining the continuity of beliefs and enriching local traditions. Culture of Indian subcontinent is said to be thousands of years old. Historians lend different versions to the genesis of subcontinental culture generally ascribing it to be the product of Indus Valley Civilization (IVC) that is dated sometime about 2600 years before Christ.

In the course of 4600 years of both oral and written history, this subcontinent has seen the rise of many religions such as Hinduism, Zoroastrianism, Buddhism and Jainism that continue to prevail even today. It also witnessed as well as adopted foreign beliefs such as Christianity, Islam and Judaism. History records that people prophesying these beliefs arrived for seeking asylum against persecution in their native lands or for commercial enterprises or with the intention of conquest.

Historians note that the subcontinent became a melting pot of religions that arrived at different times, initially producing conflicts but eventually leading to amalgamation. The synthesis and fusion of foreign beliefs produced its own variations in oral traditions. Unlike in some other parts of the world, this process enriched both native and foreign cultures. For example, we find millions of Hindus partaking in Urs festivals of Sufi saints at Hazarat Nizamuddin Dargah at Delhi, Hazarat Moinuddin Chisti Dargah at Ajmer, Hazarat Peer Fatehullah Shah Baba Dargah at Raisen (Madhya Pradesh), Hazarat Jaanpak Shaheed Dargah at Nalgonda (Telangana), and Hazarat Syed Shahul Hameed Dargah, Nagore (Tamil Nadu). We also find Muslim and Hindu devotees praying at the Church of Our Lady of Vailankanni located in Vailankanni near Nagapattinam (Tamil Nadu). When we look more closely at grassroots society, we find astounding traditions like Muslim warriors sharing the pedestal with some of the ancient deities of India. For example, at Kagam (26 km from Erode, Tamil Nadu), a Muslim Ravuttar shares the shrine of Lord Karthikey (Murugan), that too with a smoking pipe in his hand!

The Ravutta Kumarasami temple at Kagam in the heart of Kongu country, complete with a mix of small minarets, a dome, gopuram and a vimana, is testimony to shared history in a not-so-distant past, where basic human values were revered. The temple, belonging to the Kannan Kootam of Kagam, a clan which is part of the industrious Kongu Vellala Gounder community, has sculptures of Ravuttars all over it. From the arch at the entrance to the sanctum sanctorum, there are sculptures of bearded Ravuttars, either seated erect with a sword in hand or mounted on their steeds with swords drawn. And there is also a Ravuttar draped in a lungi, smoking a cigar and reclining above the doorway. Inside the sanctum sanctorum, the Ravuttars are depicted sitting majestically with raised swords next to Lord Murugan (Kumara Sami)[1].

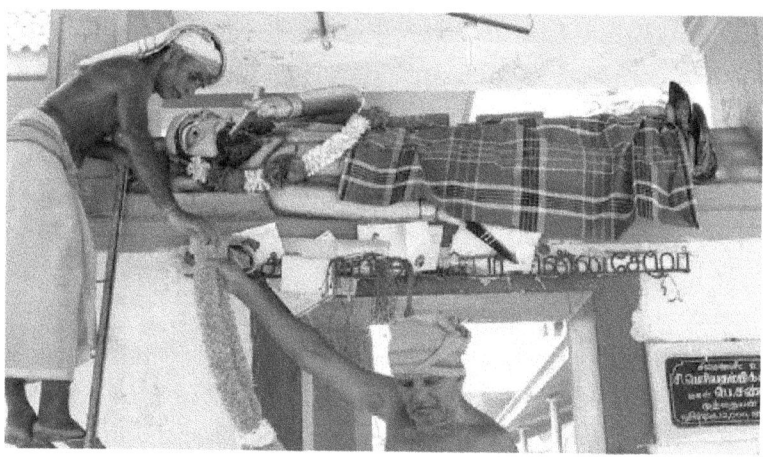

Source: The Hindu (Online). https://www.thehindu.com/society/history-and-culture/a-secular-temple-in-the-heart-of-kongu-nadu/article24103046.ece. Accessed October 26, 2023.

Elsewhere in Sri Rangam (and Tirupati and Melukote in Karnataka), we find presiding deities have even taken Muslim princess as their consorts. They are also worshipped by the most ardent of Hindu devotees. These stories of fusion have not always produced such pleasant examples of adoption and admiration. They have also produced an equal number that have prejudiced the communities against each other, lending some eerie recounts that portray nothing but villainy. Together, all these homages, pilgrimages and villainous

---

1   Anwar, Kombai S. (June 07, 2018). A secular temple in Kongu heartland: Kannan Kootam of Kaagam has Murugan and Ravuttar sharing space, The Hindu (Online). https://www.thehindu.com/society/history-and-culture/a-secular-temple-in-the-heart-of-kongu-nadu/article24103046.ece. Accessed October 26, 2023.

accounts go beyond political and sectarian discourses, for they flourish in the domain of faith that does not distinguish people or places by their archetypical religious connotations.

Cultural mosaic of subcontinent was as such enriched with 18 purana[2] that dealt in detail about origins of universe, of gods and lineages of kings that ruled its parts much before foreign faiths arrived. Matsya Purana, considered as the oldest with origins in the 1st millennia before Christ[3] talks about an avatar of Lord Vishnu in the form of a fish. This great fish engulfed the earth in its mouth to save it from sinking into the ocean of abyss. Interestingly, it also talked about temple designs, giving detailed instructions as to styles of Hindu temples such as Meru, Mandara (later Mandir) and Kailasa. It laid out guidelines on foundation, spaces within core temple where people visit, and then the spire (Vimana or Shikhara). Collective works on the building of temples and divine idols (Agama sastra or science of construction) in due course became the foundation for exquisite temple architecture that we find in the subcontinent. Agama sastra also consisted a sub-branch (shilpa sastra or the science of idol making) that provided detailed techniques for measurement, proportions, sculpting styles and selection of material for making idols and sculptures[4].

Development of science in India was umblicly connected to religious precepts, for India did not perceive both as divorced from or incidental to each other. Philosophical traditions ran parallel to physical (scientific) traditions, complimenting each other as they went along the course of time. When looked at critically, we find that Indian civilization embarked upon the discovery of science of the spirit by first exploring the elements (water, fire, earth, wind and akasa or ether) that are necessary to support life. Through this investigation, it ended up exploring the science of the spirit. After mastering the science of the spirit, it went back deeper into exploration of physical sciences, achieving stellar discoveries such as Ayurveda (medical science), Dhanur Veda (science of weapon making), astronomy, mathematics including the concept of zero, etc. Lagadha's

---

2   The 18 puranas (known as Mahapuranas) are Matsya, Vishnu, Naradiya, Padma, Garuda, Varaha, Bhagavata, Kurma, Linga, Shiva, Skanda, Agni, Brahmanda, Brahmavaivarta, Markandeya, Bhavishya, Vamana, and Brahma. These Eighteen Puranas were indexed by VR Ramachandra Dikshitar in 1951. See: Ramachandra, D. V. R. (1951). The Purana index: 1. Madras: Univ. of Madras.

3   Rocher, Ludo (1986). The Puranas. Otto Harrassowitz Verlag. ISBN 978-3447025225.

4   See Srinivasan, R (2022). Musings: A Little about Everything-On Matters of Faith, https://www.amazon.com/Matters-Faith-Musings-Little-Everything/, Pp 33-36, where I have provided some details with notes on Shilpa Sastra based on an earlier research.

Vedanga Jyotisha (dated to 1200 BCE) is the oldest work on astronomy perhaps in the world[5].

The Taittiriya Aranyaka of the Yajur Veda (1500 to 800 BCE[6]) for example, talks about the origins of water. The romanized Sanskrit version with English meaning is given below:

yo'pāṃ puṣpaṃ veda | puṣpavān prajāvan paśumān bhavati | candramā vā apāṃ puṣpam | puṣpavān prajavān paśumān bhavati | ya evaṃ veda | yo'pām-āyatanaṃ veda | āyatanavān bhavati || 1||	He who knows/understands the flowers of water, He becomes the possessor of flowers, children and cattle. Moon is indeed the flower of the water, He becomes the possessor of flowers, children and cattle. He who knows this, He who knows the source of water, (He) becomes established in himself. (1)
agnir-vā apām-āyatanam | āyatanavān bhavati | yo'gner-āyatanaṃ veda | āyatanavān bhavati | apo vā agner-āyatanam | āyatanavān bhavati | ya evaṃ veda | yo'pām-āyatanaṃ veda | āyatanavān bhavati ||2||	Fire indeed is the source (basis) of water, (He) becomes established in himself, He, who knows the basis of fire. (He) becomes established in himself. Water indeed is the source (basis) of fire, (He) becomes established in himself. He who knows this, He who knows the source of water, (He) becomes established in himself. (2)
vāyur-va apām-āyatanam | āyatanavān bhavati | yo vvyor-āyatanaṃ veda | āyatanavān bhavati | āpo vai vāyor-āyatanam | āyatanavān bhavati | ya evaṃ veda | yo'pām-āyatanaṃ veda | āyatanavan bhavati ||3||	Air indeed is the source of water, (He) becomes established in himself, He who knows the basis of air. (He) becomes established in himself. Water indeed is the source of air, (He) becomes established in himself. He who knows this, He who knows the source (basis) of water, (He) becomes established in himself. (3)

---

5   Subbarayappa, B. V. (14 September 1989). Indian astronomy: A historical perspective. In Biswas, S. K.; Mallik, D. C. V.; Vishveshwara, C. V. (eds.). Cosmic Perspectives. Cambridge University Press. pp. 25–40.

6   Witzel, Michael (2001), "Autochthonous Aryans? The Evidence from Old Indian and Iranian Texts" (PDF), Electronic Journal of Vedic Studies, 7 (3): 1–115

asau vai tapann-apām-āyatanam | āyatanavān bhavati | yo'muṣya tapata āyatanam veda | āyatanavān bhavati | āpo vā amuñya tapata āyatanam | āyatanavān bhavati | ya evaṃ veda | yo'pām-āyatanam veda | āyatanavān bhavati ||4||	Scorching sun is the source of water, (He) becomes established in himself, He who knows the source /basis of scorching sun, (He) becomes established in himself. Water is the source of scorching sun, (He) becomes established in himself. He who knows this, He who knows the source/basis of water, (He) becomes established in himself. (4)
candramā vā apām-āyatnam | āyatanavān bhavati | yaçcandramasa āyatanam veda | āyatanavān bhavati | āpo vai candramasa āyatanam | āyatanavān bhavati | ya evaṃ veda | yo'pām-āyatanam veda | āyatanavān bhavati ||5||	Moon indeed is the source of water, (He) becomes established in himself, He who knows the source/basis of moon. (He) becomes established in himself. Water is the source/basis of moon, (He) becomes established in himself. He who knows this, He who knows the source/basis of water, (He) becomes established in himself. (5)
nakṣtrāṇi vā apām āyatanam | āyatanavān bhavati | yo nakṣatrāṇam āyatanam veda | āyatanavān bhavati | āpo vai nakṣatrāṇām āyatanam | āyatanavān bhavati | ya evaṃ veda | yo'pām-āyatanam veda | āyatanavān bhavati ||6||	Stars are indeed the source of water, (He) becomes established in himself, He who knows the source/basis of stars. (He) becomes established in himself. Water indeed is the source of stars, (He) becomes established in himself. He who knows this, He who knows the source/basis of water, (He) becomes established in himself. (6)
parjanyo vā apām-āyatanam | āyatanavān bhavati | yaḥ parjanyasyāyatnam veda | āyatanavān bhavati | āpo vai parjanyasyāyatanam | āyatanavān bhavati | ya evaṃ veda | yo'pām āyatanam veda | āyatanavān bhavati ||7||	Clouds indeed are the source of water, (He) becomes established in himself, He who knows the source/basis of clouds, (He) becomes established in himself. Water is indeed the source of clouds, (mutual?) (He) becomes established in himself. He who knows this, He who knows the source of water, (He) becomes established in himself. (7)

saṃvatsaro vā apām-āyatanam | āyatavān bhavati | yas-saṃvatsarasyāyatanaṃ veda | āyatavān bhavati | āpo vai saṃvatsarasyāyatanam | āyatanavān bhavati | ya evaṃ veda | yo'psu nāvaṃ pratiṣṭhitāṃ veda | pratyeva tiṣṭhati ||8||	Rainy season (Year) is indeed the source of water, (He) becomes established in himself, He who knows the source/basis of rainy season/year, (He) becomes established in himself. Water is the source/basis of rainy season/year, (He) becomes established in himself. He who knows this, He who knows that there is a raft is available, Becomes established in that raft. (8)

Source: https://periva.proboards.com/thread/7532/mantra-pushpam-meaning

It may be noted from these verses that fire, air, Sun, Moon, Air, Stars, clouds and rains are identified as sources of water that gives life, produces flowers (to be understood as grain) and food for cattle that are the source of wealth. From modern science, we do know that these are indeed the origin and source of water after extensive tests through enormous labs.

A remarkable and pertinent point to note about Indian civilization is that it intricately weaves sciences into the fabric of religion. Even today in every household and temple where devotional rites are performed, Mantra Pushpam is recited. It is recited to offer flowers to god, while it actually signifies and celebrates the origin and source of life itself! Thus, oral tradition in India must be understood as a means to teach science to people, liberally portrayed as religious practices. It must be noted that an elevated consciousness viewing science as a means to explore origins and purpose of life itself was birthed through millennia of evolution of Indian society.

This elevated consciousness perhaps was the reason why physical conquests were considered inferior to conquest of the spirit in the subcontinent. That is the reason why we find great emperors and kings of India willingly and voluntarily submitting to sages and learned men of their time. Despite having reached the pinnacles of glory as emperors, they even aspired to become great saints. Some examples would be in order at this juncture.

1. From Ramayana, we find the story of Vishwamitra, a great king and an immensely powerful warrior. He once went hunting in the jungle and was afflicted with thirst. He wandered into the hermitage of Sage Vasishta, a great saint of the time who was also the guru of the Kingdom of Ayodhya.

Finding the king in a tired and distressed state, Sage Vasishta offered water, fruits and sumptuous feast to the king and his entire army. The king noticed that this humble hermitage feasted an entire army with the grace of a holy cow, Shabala (Kamadenu). It appeared to possess powers to grant every wish. Noting this, Vishwamitra demanded that the cow be given to him so as to take care of his kingdom. Sage Vasishta declined. Enraged, the king sent his soldiers to take the cow away. To his utter surprise, it defended herself with soldiers produced from its person. Unwilling to accept this, Vishwamitra embarked on war with the sage. He shot holiest of arrows only to find that the sage had planted his 'dhanda' (the arm rest saints and mendicants use to rest their arm while using the rosary for meditation) in front. The 'dhanda' absorbed even the mightiest of his arrows. Finally, Vishwamitra dispatched 'Brahmastra' considered to be a boon from Lord Brahma himself. The 'dhanda' absorbed the brahmastra too. Defeated and crest fallen, he cried:

'Dhig balaṁ kṣatriyabalaṁ brahmatejo balaṁ balam, ekena brahma daṇḍena sarvāstrāṇi hatāni me/ tad etat samavekṣyāhaṁ prasannen driyamānasaḥ, tapo mahat samāsthāsye yad vai brahmatvakārakam[7] *(It is a shame to proclaim that power rests in the weapons of a Kshatriya. True power originates from the spiritual prowess of sages).*

Vishwamitra then renounced his kingship and performed penance to attain spiritual powers. He was eventually satisfied only when Sage Vasishta proclaimed him as brahma rishi (a saint who has attained eternal bliss and therefore the knowledge of brahma).

2. From the story of Asoka the great we find that a colossal war in Kalinga eventually drove him to renounce worldly attachments and set about governing his vast empire through 'dharma'[8]. Asoka is credited by historians as one of the greatest emperors in history for his contribution to the spread of dharma.
3. From the story Barthruhari[9], we find that this great king of Bhoj was

---

7   Sarga 56, Bala Kanda, Valmiki Ramayana.
8   Dharma denotes the concept of righteousness.
9   Barthruhari is dated by historians to 5th century AD, between 425 and 510, if not earlier. See: Harold G. Coward; Karl H. Potter; K. Kunjunni Raja, eds. (1990), Encyclopedia of Indian philosophies: The philosophy of the grammarians, Motilal Banarsidass Publ., p. 121, ISBN 978-81-208-0426-5 & Saroja Bhate; Johannes Bronkhorst, eds. (1994), Bhartṛhari, philosopher and grammarian: Proceedings of the First International Conference on Bhartṛhari (University of Poona, January 6–8, 1992),

renowned for exceptional power and administrative prowess. It is said that he remained restless despite the accolades showered on him and the prosperity of his kingdom. Haunted by his restless mind, he was standing at the balcony of his palace one night. A night watchman on patrol was heard approaching. To his surprise, the king found this watchman singing what appeared to be a sloka through which people were cautioned to stay alert. The watchman cried:

क्षणँ वित्तँ क्षणँ चित्तँ क्षणँ जीवितिमावयोःऽयमस्य करूणा नास्ततिस्मात् जाग्रत जाग्रत ॥[10]

> *Money, memory and life are all momentary.*
> *Lord Yama, the lord of death, does not show any mercy. Therefore be awake!!*

In a flash, Barthruhari realized the folly of pursuit of human happiness and gave up his kingly life to become a mendicant. He went on to compose grammar, Sringara Sataka, Neeti Sataka and Vairagya Sataka that are of foundational value to all the schools of philosophy in the subcontinent.

4. From Chatrapati Shivaji and Saint Tukaram, we find that this great saint[11] (1598-1649) molded Maratha consciousness and was considered the guru of Chatrapati Shivaji. Scholars note that the legacy of Tukaram and bhakti movement of saints 'during this period of Hindu-Muslim wars, as transforming language of shared religion, and religion a shared language. It is they who helped to bind the Marathas together against the Mughals on the basis not of any religious ideology but of a territorial cultural identity'.[12]

5. From the story of Swami Vidyaranya and Vijayanagara Empire's founders Harihara and Bukka, we find that the ideals of service to country was

---

Motilal Banarsidass Publ., p. 21, ISBN 978-81-208-1198-0.

10 This sloka is part of the composition by Adi Shankara's Vairagya Sloka comprising of seven stanzas. The version of Bathruhari narrated here is what I have heard and wondered as to how Adishankara's recitalsome 400 years after Barthruhari came to be ascribed to a watchman. It can only be deduced that the impermanence of human life being a pivotal precept in the Vedic philosophy that originated over 2000 years before Barthruhari, the cry of the watchman must have been of similar meaning. This is yet another example of oral traditions that mutate and intermingle with local lore.

11 Richard M. Eaton (2005), A Social History of the Deccan, 1300–1761: Eight Indian Lives, Cambridge University Press, ISBN 978-0521716277, pages 138-141

12 Chitre, Dilip (1991), Tuka: Selected Poetry of Tukaram, Penguin, ISBN 978-0140445978, Pp. xvi-xvii

interwoven with bhakti and cultural traditions inherited from ancient times. This book has a separate chapter on Swami Vidyaranya and the founding of Vijayanagara Empire.

Each of these and many other narratives in cultural and religious domain of the subcontinent have their origins in history, influenced by the life and times of people in flesh and blood. It may be argued that events of the time influenced them to take courses that they took. Their actions in turn engendered myths and belief. However, it must be recognized that cause leads to action that produces further cause in an everlasting cycle. We may even take Newton's 3rd Law to support this thought. As time rolls by, these oral narratives embellish cultural belief with their own additions and alterations, some based on facts and yet others based on hearsay. However, they weave themselves into the cultural mosaic of a society so much so that they become inseparable from actual history and contribute to the strengthening of social consciousness.

A classical and interesting example as to how real events give rise to oral traditions may be worth examining here.

It was with the work of French orientalist, Antoine Galland and Hanna Diyab the Syrian Christian in the eighteenth century, that the first full-scale translation of *One Thousand and One Nights* took place. Between 1704-1717, Galland rendered 'Alf Layla wa Layla' (the first Arabic Version) into French as 'Les Mille et Une Nuits'. The Nights took on another life here with Galland's inclusion of new material 'orphan stories' that have become synonymous with the Nights in Western culture. This includes Aladdin and the Story of Magic Lamp and Ali Baba and the Fourty Thieves. The origin of these 'orphan stories' has long perplexed historians of the Nights until most recently – the latest discovery of Hanna Diyab's memoirs, translated into English as The Book of Travels, demonstrates his authorship of these popular tales, a revelation that serves to further nuance the complex ties between French and Arabic literary history[13].

The Arabian Nights is one of the most widely read and vividly recounted stories in the world that continue to amaze and amuse readers. The story of Aladdin and Magic Lamp has been reproduced in other books, comics, theatre,

---

13 Zagot, Dr. Shazia (JANUARY 11, 2023). A very short history of One Thousand and One Nights, https://www.shakespearesglobe.com/discover/blogs-and-features/2023/01/11/a-very-short-history-of-one-thousand-and-one-nights/#:~:text=Its%20roots%20lie%20both%20in,through%20an%20Arabic%20literary%20tradition. Accessed November 02, 2023.

pantomime, musical theatre, and of course in dozens of Hollywood movies. It has also been translated widely into nearly every living language in the world.

It may be recalled from the story that Aladdin was taken to a cave by a wizard who wanted to obtain immense wealth stored in there. Aladdin discovers the treasure but then gets trapped in the cave. He accidentally rubs a lamp and a Jinni appears before him. The Jinni brings him out together with amazing treasures stored in the cave, making him rich. The rest of the story is well known.

What is of importance to us is the description of the treasure. It is said to contain unaccountable number of gold ingots, precious stones, jewels, coins and silver. There were also bales of silken cloth and other valuables.

Antoine Galland added these descriptions in around 17th century. While meriting compelling imagination, historians note that riches described there were the result of Malik Kafur's loot from Sri Rangam and Madurai[14]. Charles Allen notes that the description of wealth in Arabian Nights was influenced by the exploits of Muslim invaders in the 10th to 13th century in Southern India. The story of plunder apparently travelled through the Silk Route becoming immortalized through brilliant narrations in West Asian local traditions.

This shows that oral traditions and real history invariably influence each other. Therefore, it is important for us to bear in mind that oral traditions should not be merely dubbed as superstitious or figs of imagination. They need to be carefully studied through historical evidence to arrive at their source. This examination may help us to understand how culture evolves to become a necessary factor in integrating faith with history.

Oral tradition that carries stories of events has been acknowledged as a powerful medium, akin to the internet (but only older) that has influenced, shaped and sustained cultures across many continents[15]. Recognizing the importance of oral traditions, United Nations adopted a Convention for the Safeguarding of the Intangible Cultural Heritage in 2003[16]. Article 2 of the Convention defines oral traditions as:

The "intangible cultural heritage", as defined in paragraph 1 above, is manifested inter alia in the following domains:

---

14 Allen, Charles (2017). Coromandal: A Personal History, London: Little, Brown p 237.

15 Britannica (n.d.). Oral Tradition. https://www.britannica.com/topic/oral-tradition, Accessed October 26, 2023.

16 UNESCO (Nov 03, 2003). Convention for the Safeguarding of the Intangible Cultural Heritage. https://ich.unesco.org/en/convention#art2 Accessed October 26, 2023.

a. Oral traditions and expressions, including language as a vehicle of the intangible cultural heritage;
b. Performing arts;
c. Social practices, rituals and festive events;
d. Knowledge and practices concerning nature and the universe;
e. Traditional craftsmanship.

Part III of the Convention stipulates that the state parties to the convention shall:

a. Take the necessary measures to ensure the safeguarding of the intangible cultural heritage present in its territory;
b. among the safeguarding measures referred to in Article 2, paragraph 3, identify and define the various elements of the intangible cultural heritage present in its territory, with the participation of communities, groups and relevant non-governmental organizations. (Article 11).

It further stipulates in Article 13 (c) that states shall 'foster scientific, technical and artistic studies, as well as research methodologies, with a view to effective safeguarding of the intangible cultural heritage, in particular the intangible cultural heritage in danger'.

The importance of oral traditions and the need to preserve, investigate and interrogate history as a tool for preserving culture has been acclaimed by many scholarly studies. Scholars have also questioned the validity of such oral traditions as reliable sources. They note that from the time of Jan Vansina's 'Oral Tradition' in 1965, such debates have been part of academic scrutiny[17]. For example, in Canada, in a study pertaining to oral traditions, some incisive questions were posed in following terms:

> *Compelling questions are being raised- in the mass media, in museum exhibits, and in both popular and academic writings – about how historical depictions of cross-cultural encounters are constructed and gain authority. One issue in these debates concerns the status of indigenous oral traditions, specifically how oral traditions can contribute to documenting the varieties of historical understanding in areas of the world where written documents are either relatively recent or even absent. In many ways, historians and*

---

17 Hamilton, C. A. (1987). Ideology and Oral Traditions: Listening to the Voices "From Below." History in Africa, 14, 67–86. https://doi.org/10.2307/3171833

anthropologists are converging in their approaches to historical reconstruction, pointing to the need to unite anthropological attention to cultural categories, cosmologies, and symbols with historians' disciplined control of written records? A related question, though, concerns who gets to frame and to tell the story- whose voices are prominent in these discussions and whose are marginalized. Increasingly, indigenous peoples are demanding that their oral traditions be taken seriously as legitimate perspectives on history. The issue, for them, centres on who controls the images and the representations of their lives portrayed to the larger world. While there is growing awareness in Canada about the need to re-evaluate the history of Native-white relations, it is clear that Aboriginal peoples' views of their own history rarely appear in academic literature. This debate is as much about epistemology as about authorship. Indigenous people who grow up immersed in oral tradition frequently suggest that their narratives are better understood by absorbing the successive personal messages revealed to listeners in repeated tellings than by trying to analyse and publicly explain their meanings. This contrasts with a scholarly approach which encourages close scrutiny of texts and which contends that by openly addressing conflicting interpretations, we may illuminate subtle meanings and enrich our understanding?

The challenge, then, is to acknowledge this dilemma without dismissing it as insoluble, to respect both the legitimate claims of First Nations to tell their own stories and the moral and scholarly obligation to write culturally grounded histories that can help us learn from the past[18].

Even though the scholarly merit of orally told histories has been much debated across the world, it is acknowledged that oral traditions are vital to fostering culture and they play an important role in strengthening of the cultural roots and sense of belonging.

When we look at the subcontinent, we find immense evidence for this. As a matter of fact, the Vedas held as the very soul of Hinduism originated from oral traditions and carried down millennia only by oral transmission. That is the reason they are known as *Sruti* (that which is heard). Even the purana are known as *Smruti* (that which is passed down through recitals from memory). From its origins in about 2600 years before Christ, the mere volume of Rig Veda[19] carried

---

18   Cruikshank, J. (1994). Oral Tradition and Oral History: Reviewing Some Issues. The Canadian Historical Review 75(3), 403-418. https://www.muse.jhu.edu/article/574633.

19   Rig-Veda Samhita is the core text with a collection of 10 books with 1,028 hymns in about 10,600 verses.

through oral recitation is testimony that in India oral recital and tradition carry much more weight than written tradition generally seen in the Arab and Western world. Even the epics, Ramayana and Mahabharata have been part of oral traditions of India. Ramayana alone consists of 24000 verses and Mahabharata, 200000. It is then to be recognized that oral traditions have a strong root and influence over the social and culture fabric of this huge subcontinent.

Foreign invasions beginning with Alexander the Great, Persians, Afghans and Europeans later, intermingled with native culture and produced more orally counted and recounted instances. They in their turn led to the formation as well as destruction of beliefs and practices who, in their entirety compose the cultural mosaic of this subcontinent.

The next section provides a concise version of history of India relevant to the narratives as a contextual setting for this book.

This book deals with fifteen of narratives based on oral renditions that have deep roots in southern part of India. Many of these stories are part of household lore. This book steps beyond the commonly known oral versions without ignoring them. What it does first is to take each of them and study the historical context in which they occurred. Secondly, it investigates the historical contexts with corroborative evidences from scholarly sources. Thirdly, it apportions to each of the stories as much credibility to the extent historical evidences permit.

The objective is not to credit or discredit the oral narrations. It is neither to celebrate nor vilify a historical person, but only to see whether the oral narration stands the testimony of history. It is an attempt to stitch together the gaps and voids in the narrations so as to see if they receive support from archao-historical records.

Each of the stories relate to a temple in South India. Towards the end of the book, three stories have been included that relate to Colonial times.

I do hope that this modest attempt promotes inquisitive and evidence based historiographical studies and contributes to the strengthening of this amazing cultural fabric of India which AL Basham fondly called 'A Wonder that was India'.

Historical Context

The Ranganathaswamy temple at Sri Rangam, near Trichirapalli in Tamil Nadu or (Trichy as it is popularly known) is at the heart of the Vaishnavite culture that pervades southern parts of India. The temple is said to be thousands of years old. While legends and literary evidence support such ancient origins, its significance to South Indian history is more datable, though curiously less explored. Historians like Sarcar place origin of the stone inscriptions in the temple to about 100 BCE and 100 AD[20].

Earliest references to Sri Rangam as the abode of Ranganathaswamy date back to 785 BCE. It has been part of Alzvar Divyaprabandam (the bhakti compositions of the 12 Vaishnavite saints of Tamil country). The deity has been affectionately referred to as Ranga, Azhagiya Manavala and a thousand other names. It is also a place where the greatest of devotees, Andal, lived and attained her union with the Lord. This story centres on events in early 14th century when it faced invasion by external forces, perhaps for the first time in its history, giving rise to the oral narratives that are the focus of this book.

From ancient times, Tamil country was ruled by three dynasties - the Chola, Chera and Pandya. Folklore, literary and archaeo-historical records also say the Pandya as being the oldest among these three dynasties. Archaeological excavations at Adichanallur near Thoothukudi (Tuticorin) and in Tamirabarani River delta reveal ancient Greek and Roman connections to Pandya. Megasthenese of 323 BCE, Ptolemy of 47 BCE and Periplus[21] refer to Pandya and extensive trade with

---

20 Sircar, D.C. (1979). Some Epigraphical Records of the Medieval Period from Eastern India. Delhi: Shakti Malik. ISBN 9788170170969.

21 The amount of Roman trade passing through Red Sea ports was upped dramatically when Roman Emperor Augustus (r. 27 BCE - 14 CE) brought Egypt under Roman control in 30 BCE. The Greek geographer, philosopher, and historian Strabo reported that "in his day 120 vessels sailed regularly from Egypt to India, whereas previously very few made the journey" (Geography, 16.4). https://www.worldhistory.org/Periplus_of_the_Erythraean_Sea/

Greece in pearls and woven silks. The ports of Muziris[22] (Musiri or Muchiri in Tamil) and Korkai (the port where Tamirabarani River enters the Bay of Bengal) find extensive mention in Greek-Roman records. Tamil country had almost never faced invasions of the kind that visited its northern neighbors.

Invasions in North India

In the north, Alexander the Great is said to be the first to arrive at the banks of the Indus and defeat Porus in 326 BC at Hydespas. But history shows that Darius I, the emperor of Persia, was indeed the first one to reach the banks of Indus River in 515 BCE. Ali Mousavi noted that the exploits of Darius are recorded in the foundation tablets of Apadana Palace as below:

> *Darius the great king, king of kings, king of countries, son of Hystaspes, an Achaemenid. King Darius says: This is the kingdom which I hold, from the Sacae who are beyond Sogdia to Kush, and from Sind ("Hidauv", locative of "Hiduš", i.e. "Indus valley") to Lydia (Old Persian: "Spardâ") – [this is] what Ahuramazda, the greatest of gods, bestowed upon me. May Ahuramazda protect me and my royal house!*
>
> *—DPh inscription of Darius I in the foundations of the Apadana Palace*[23]

Darius again invaded Indus valley in 514 duly followed later by his successor, Xerxes. Darius is said to have controlled the territory from Gandhara (Kandahar) in Afghanistan to Karachi in present day Pakistan. Alexander the Great merely followed him two hundred years later.

First Muslim invaders also came from Persia. Muhammad ibn al-Qāsim al-Thaqafī an Arab military commander in the service of Umayyad Caliphate conquered Sindh. He ruled Sindh from 712 to 715 AD.

Three hundred years after Mohammad bin Qasim came Muhammad of

---

22   First major spice trade center in the world. Located in the Indian State of Kerala on the southwestern coast of India. The exact location is not known. Probably established by 3000 BCE, it remained one of India's most important trading ports through the Roman period. In the Akananuru, a collection of ancient Tamil poetry, it was described as "the city where the beautiful vessels, the masterpieces of the Yavanas [westerners], stir white foam on the Periyar, river of Kerala, arriving with gold and departing with pepper" (Perur, 2016). https://www.worldhistory.org/Periplus_of_the_Erythraean_Sea/

23   Mousavi, Al (2012). Persepolis: Discovery and After Life of a World Wanderer, Boston: Walter de Gryuter, Pp. 171-172.

Ghazni, ruler of Ghazni in Afghanistan. He is part of north Indian lore. He ruled Ghazni in Afghanistan from 998 to 1030. Ghazni Mohammed as he is known in India invaded and looted extensive areas in the Gangetic plains as well as upto Malwa (Rajasthan and Gujarat). It is said that he invaded 17 times and each time, he looted Somnath and Dwarka in Gujarat. However, he did not cross the Narmada River.

Mohammed of Ghor or Ghori Mohammed as he is known in India, ruled from Ghor (Afghanistan). His raids into the heart of north India actually laid the foundations for later Muslim invasions. He defeated Prithviraj Chauhan of Ajmer/Delhi in the 2nd Battle of Tarain in 1192 virtually ending the rule of Hindu kings from Delhi. He too did not venture beyond Narmada River.

Mohammad of Ghor appointed Qutbuddin Aibak as his governor of Delhi in 1194, after the battle of Tarain. Aibak in due course became the first ruling sultan of Delhi. Aibak ruled Delhi till 1210. While playing polo in Lahore He fell from his horse and died. In succession after succession in the next eight decades, Allauddin Khilji ascended to the throne of Delhi in October 1296.

Banarsi Prasad Saxena records that Allauddin Khilji had heard of the immense wealth of Hindu kingdoms that lay beyond Narmada River during his campaign in Bhilsa[24]. This historian even records that Allauddin kept this matter a secret from his sovereign so as to take up a campaign at a suitable time later[25].

It is important to note that these expeditions did not result in permanent suzerainty over northern territories till the Delhi Sultanate was founded by Qutbuddin Aibak. Therefore they appear to have been undertaken for some short-term gains initially.

Invaders from the time of Mohammad Qasim were driven by iconoclastic ideals that considered destruction of idols of Hindus as a sacred duty. Ghazi Salar Masud, Ghori and Ghazni remain the highlights of such a fervour with repeated destruction of temples in Mathura, Ayodhya, Ujjain and Somnath, to mention only a few. Ghazni's seventeen invasions to loot Somnath in particular, are part of Indian lore. Their exploits will be dealt in brief detail in later chapters.

---

24 Saksena, Banarsi Prasad (1992) [1970]. The Khaljis: Alauddin Khalji. In Mohammad Habib and Khaliq Ahmad Nizami (ed.). A Comprehensive History of India: The Delhi Sultanat (A.D. 1206–1526). Vol. 5 (Second ed.)

25 Habibullah, ABM. (1992) [1970]. The Khaljis: Jalaluddin Khalji. In Mohammad Habib; Khaliq Ahmad Nizami (eds.). A Comprehensive History of India. Vol. 5: The Delhi Sultanat (A.D. 1206–1526). The Indian History Congress / People's Publishing House.

These affairs continued unabated almost till the founding of Mughal Empire by Babur. Iconoclastic objectives of earlier rulers became moderate in Mughal times, especially under Akbar the Great who embraced all faiths. He abolished jiziya, a tax that was imposed on Hindu pilgrims from the times of Allauddin Khilji. Akbar even propagated a faith of his own, Din-e-Ilahi, which synthesised the belief of all faiths. It did not gain popularity and ended with Akbar himself. There were barely 19 followers at the time of Aurangzeb, who in any case was opposed to it. However to a great extent, this legacy of tolerance was continued by Jahangir and Shah Jahan, after Akbar. Shah Jahan's elder son, Dara Shikoh, spent many years at Varanasi learning Hindu philosophy and even translated fifty Upanishads into Persian. 'Majma '-ul-Bahrain: Or, The Mingling of the Two Oceans' by Prince Dara Shikoh is considered to be a classical work. It says Dara commissioned a translation of Yoga Vasishtha after he had Lord Ram appear and embrace him in a dream. Dara's activities were one of the prime reasons for Aurangzeb to have him killed, as he was an ardent believer in the supremacy of Islam over other faiths. As emperor, he had the jiziya re-imposed. He demolished the Vishwanath Temple at Varanasi and built Gyan Vapi mosque in its place.

This historical setting of the affairs of the north are important to the narratives in this book as each story commences from the raid of Malik Kafur to the southern parts of India. He was a slave general of Allauddin Khilji.

Having plotted history of invasions in the north briefly, it is necessary to revert to South India.

South India: 9th to 14th Century

The kings of Tamil lands (Pandya, Chola and Chera) were popularly referred to as Mummudi i.e. three-crowned. Historically this refers to one of the three dynasties gaining upper hand and claiming in the process, the crown of other two viz., wearing three crowns. But they mostly limited their territorial ambitions to the geographical limits of Deccan. Even there, they confined their ambitions to the south of Krishna River, in general. Literary evidence points to Chola kings taking expeditions to the north, defeating Kalinga (Odisha) or even king of Varanasi. Chola even used a title 'Gangai Kondan' (the conqueror of Ganges) to symbolize their northern conquests. History finds that the Chola named their capital 'Gangaikonda Cholapuram' after these conquests. Historians record that Gangaikonda Cholapuram served as capital of Chola for nearly 250 years from 1025 AD. Located in Ariyalur district of Tamil Nadu, it is now a UNESCO heritage centre famous for the architectural wonders in temple construction of the Chola period. The expeditions of Chola did not result in permanent suzerainty over any territory in the north.

Even Asoka the Great who nearly conquered the four corners of subcontinent in 2nd century BC stopped short of Pandya territories. He made liberal reference in his edicts to Pandya as the ruler of southern parts. This scenario prevailed almost till 4th century AD when Pallava dynasty (275 to 897 AD) from Telugu speaking parts north of Krishna River arrived at Kanchipuram. Historians like Krishnaswamy Aiyangar state that Pallava belonged to Thondai Mandalam[26] (roughly the Arcot/Kanchipuram region extending into the Nellore district of Andhra Pradesh). Herman Kulke and Dietmar Rothmund, on the other hand, believed that Pallava were descendants of Ashwathama (of Mahabharata fame, son of Dronacharya, who ruled Panchala as per Mahabharata), taking the lineage of Pallava to the period of Mahabharata itself. The Pallava were ambitious and expanded their dominion over Mummudi territories, subjugated Sri Lanka and set about trading with Southeast Asia. Mahendravarma I (600–630) and Narasimhavarma I (Mamalla) (630–668) of Pallava are the most notable kings of this dynasty. Mahendravarma was defeated by Pulakesin II of Chalukya sometime around 622 AD. His son, Narasimhavarma defeated Pulakesin II by taking the battle to Vatapi (present day Badami in Karnataka), killed him and even laid the city to waste[27].

Pulakesin II is also noted to have successfully repulsed the first ever naval expedition by the Caliphate to conquer and proselytize in South India. The 2nd Caliph, Umar-bin-Akhtab despatched a naval force under Usman of the tribe of Sakif to capture and occupy the west coast on India. Usman's naval forces were routed by the navy of Pulakesin II, pushing them back to Oman[28].

The fall of Pallava in 897 AD reverted the contest for South India among the Mummudi i.e. Chola, Chera and Pandya. While Pandya-Chola-Chera rivalries lasted for millennia thereafter, the real contest for dominions arose in the 11th century AD. South of the Narmada River, Yadava of Devagiri (1187–1317 AD) had risen as a substantial power that could even check invasions from north.

---

26 Mahalingam, TV (1969). Kāñcīpuram in early South Indian history. Asia Pub. House, p. 22.
27 Eraly, Abraham (2011). The First Spring: The Golden Age of India. Penguin Books India. ISBN 978-0-670-08478-4.
28 Mishra, Dr. Ram Gopal (December 1992). Indian Resistance to Early Muslim Invaders Up to 1206 A.D., New Delhi: Anu Books, p. 121. ISBN 978-8193608883.

To their east, Kakatiya of Warangal (1163-1323 AD) were powerful contestants permanently engaged in wars with Yadava. To their south, Pandya (1101-1345 AD), by now reduced in power, were in perennial contest with Chera (who were as such restricted to the coastal regions of present day Kerala[29]), Chola and Hoysala who threatened them from across the Eastern Ghats. It is a historical irony that in 1310, even as Malik Kafur defeated Kakatiya at Warangal and proceeded to subjugate Hoysala of Dwarasamudra, two sons of the Pandya king Maravarman Kulasekhara Pandya, Veera and Sundara, were locked in a contest for the throne of Madurai. This contest provided the perfect setting for Malik Kafur to descend to Madurai, looting Sri Rangam and Chidambaram enroute. It was sardonic that Sundara Pandya III went to the extent of inviting Malik Kafur to assist him in the contest for throne[30]. Apparently, he did not truly foresee the consequences that would change the history of South India forever.

History reveals that Yadava of Devagiri who geographically were the closest to the Narmada also did not envision the kind of events that would take place when Allauddin Khilji set himself as sultan of Delhi. Nor were they prepared for the onslaught that Malik Kafur would bring upon them.

Malik Kafur, known as Taj al-Din Izz al-Dawla, incidentally was a Hindu slave bought for a thousand Dinars by Allauddin's general Nusrat Khan during a raid in Gujarat in 1299. Kafur is also known as Hazar Dinari, referring to the amount that was paid by his purchaser.

Malik Kafur was a eunuch[31].

Temples and Muhammadan Invasions

While the affairs of the north remained turbulent, regions below Narmada River were unaffected till Allauddin Khilji set his eyes on the wealth of the south. In 1296, he descended upon Devagiri where an unsuspecting Ramachandra Yadava resisted him valiantly, but conceded after Devagiri was subjected to a prolonged siege. While Allauddin reinstated him as a vassal, immense loot was obtained from Yadava[32]. Allauddin then turned his attention on Kakatiya of Warangal

---

29   By 1100, the great Chera of yester years were practically part of history.

30   Aiyangar, S Krishnaswamy (1921). South India and Her Muhammadan Invaders, London: Humphrey Milford Oxford University Press. Pp. 43-131.

31   Jackson, Peter (2003). The Delhi Sultanate: A Political and Military History. Cambridge University Press. ISBN 978-0-521-54329-3.

32   Saksena, Banarsi Prasad (1992) [1970]. The Khaljis: Alauddin Khalji. In Mohammad Habib

ruled by Prataparudra. However, he was distracted to Delhi as the Mongol of Chagatai clan had invaded his northern borders. Allauddin defeated them in the battle of Kili in 1298-99[33]. After onsolidating his victories, he re-launched a campaign against Chittor and Warangal in 1302-03. Kakatiya of Warangal did not submit so easily and the monsoons proved to be a greater challenge. Khilji was to face a defeat yet again. Again, part of the reason was another invasion of Mongols in 1303[34]. He returned to Delhi, only to face one more Mongol invasion in 1305. Both the Mongol invasions were successfully checked, but the plans for south had to wait. In 1308 he commissioned Malik Kafur to lead the ransacking of the south. Kafur initially arrived at Devagiri, obtained both huge wealth and support of Yadava to invade Kakatiya territories. In February-March 1310, after a month long siege, Prataparudra of Warangal submitted to Malik Kafur with a huge ransom including the famous Koh-I-Noor diamond[35].

Learning at Warangal of the prosperity of Hoysala and Pandya, Malik Kafur turned further south. He defeated Ballala II of Hoysala at Dwarasamudra and then went for Pandya of Madurai. On the way, he looted Sri Rangam temple and Chidambaram before proceeding to seize Madurai. Historians note that Sundara Pandya sought his help in his struggle for the throne of Madurai at this time. However, he appeared to have changed his mind and led a force to check Malik Kafur. He was caught in the battle on the banks of Cauvery River and slain to death. As Kafur reached Madurai, he was challenged by an uncle of the Pandya, Vikrama Pandya who defeated him in battle. He however managed to obtain a ransom of 96000 gold coins and half the number of elephants and horses in return for not sacking Madurai[36]. Developments at Delhi were a major reason for Malik Kafur's compromise at Madurai and hasty return to Delhi.

---

and Khaliq Ahmad Nizami (ed.). A Comprehensive History of India: The Delhi Sultanat (A.D. 1206–1526). Vol. 5 (Second ed.). The Indian History Congress / People's Publishing House, Pp. 322-323.

33 Lal, Kishori Saran (1950). History of the Khaljis (1290-1320). Allahabad: The Indian Press, Pp. 159-161.

34 Ibid. Pp. 164-165.

35 Saksena, Banarsi Prasad (1992) [1970]. The Khaljis: Alauddin Khalji. In Mohammad Habib and Khaliq Ahmad Nizami (ed.). A Comprehensive History of India: The Delhi Sultanat (A.D. 1206–1526). Vol. 5 (Second ed.). The Indian History Congress / People's Publishing House, Pp. 409-410.

36 Talbot, Cynthia (2001). Precolonial India in Practice: Society, Religion and Identity in Andhra, New York: Oxford University Press & Sastri, KAN (2023) (4th Edn). A History of South India: From Prehistoric Times to the fall of Vijayanagara, New Delhi: Oxford University Press, Pp. 197, 207-209.

Malik Kafur returned to Delhi with huge cache of wealth that is said to have exceeded the imagination of anyone else in history. Allauddin Khilji was immensely pleased and ordered some portions of the treasures from south distributed to his nobles and the army. Exploits of Malik Kafur endeared him to Khilji in more ways than the amirs (counsellors) in the court could accept. The discontent led to the murder of Allauddin Khilji by the amirs. But Malik Kafur managed to quell the affairs and assumed full powers. He even had Khilji's son, Mubharak Khilji blinded and queen imprisoned. He installed his favourite on the throne, in preference to Mubharak Khilji. These events led to further conspiracies by amirs. Malik Kafur himself was murdered by the nobles at the court in 1316. The power struggle that followed lasted for four years and Khilji were replaced by Ghias Uddin Tughlaq in 1320. He ruled as sultan till 1325.

In 1321, Ghias Uddin sent his son Ulugh Khan (later known as Muhammad bin Tughlaq) to again subjugate Yadava, Kakatiya and Hoysala who had used the power struggles at Delhi to denounce their fidelity to the sultan[37].

Ulugh Khan campaigned in the south for nearly four years. After bringing Yadava back as vassals to Delhi, he laid siege to Warangal in 1323. Initially repulsed by Prataparudra, he rebounded to conquer Warangal and despatched Prataparudra as a prisoner to Delhi. Prataparudra however ended his own life on the banks of Narmada, not willing to be insulted at Delhi. Kakatiya dynasty perished forever after this incident. Having subjugated Warangal, Ulugh Khan proceeded to Dwarasamudra, defeated Hoysala and turned his attention on Madurai. He took Madurai, looted the town and temple.

Before returning to Delhi with sumptuous loot, he installed Jalal Uddin Ahsan Khan as a governor to look after territories in the south. By 1327, Ulugh Khan had effectively conquered entire South India. But by 1335, Jalal Uddin Ahsan Khan proclaimed himself as sultan of Madurai. This sultanate lasted till 1378, when Vijayanagara forces led by Kumara Kampana (son of Bukka I) defeated them and installed their own Nayak to rule Madurai.

Vijayanagara Empire founded by Harihara I and Bukka I in 1336 at Anegundi (later Vijayanagara) became the largest Hindu empire of the time. It was successful in checkmating Muslim forces from the north as a bulwark against invasions till 1565. However, the combined armies of Bhamani Sultans (Bijapur, Berar, Bidar, Golconda and Ahmadnagar) defeated Rama Raya of

---

37 Sastri, KAN (2023) (4th Edn). A History of South India: From Prehistoric Times to the fall of Vijayanagara, New Delhi: Oxford University Press, p. 211.

Vijayanagara in the battle of Talikotta (Talaikottai) in January 1565 thus ending the empire. The Nayak appointed by Vijayanagara in the territories controlled by them (Vellore, Senji, Tanjore, Madurai, etc.) continued to hold sway till 1646 as kings in their own right.

Though Bhamani Sultans united against their common foe i.e. Vijayanagara, they also fought among themselves and switched loyalties to the Mughal emperor as suited to their circumstances. While the later rulers of sultanates like Tanah Shah (1672-1699) of Golconda displayed considerable respect for other faiths, most of the sultans were driven by iconoclastic fervour witnessed in earlier times.

Studies about these Muslim sultans and conquerors provide a vastly different account of the temples destroyed or vandalized by them. Some websites even claim the number to be in excess of 60000[38]. Richard Eaton, a noted professor of history, in an interview with Ajaz Ashraf for Scroll Magazine, commenting on his own study pointing to the destruction of 80 temples[39], said:

> *I have no doubt that more than 80 temples were desecrated by Muslims, just as there were probably more temples desecrated by Hindus than are in the record. Again, to quote myself, "Undoubtedly some temples were desecrated but the facts in the matter were never recorded, or the facts were recorded but the records themselves no longer survive. Conversely, later Indo-Muslim chroniclers, seeking to glorify the religious zeal of earlier Muslim rulers, sometimes attributed acts of temple desecration to such rulers even when no contemporary evidence supports the claims."*[40]

As observed by Eaton himself, it is impossible to provide an accurate account or even to hazard an estimate. Many of the occurrences where substantial booty is mentioned are derived from court historians and poets like Nuruddin Barani, Firishta and the travelogues of Nuniz, etc. While such sources testify the occurrence, it is difficult to take indicated volumes as correct as these writers worked in the courts of sultans concerned. Poetic exaggeration in order to please their sovereign, therefore needs to be kept in mind.

---

38   See: https://organiser.org/2019/07/09/124265/bharat/islamic-destruction-of-hindu-temples-2/

39   Eaton, Richard (January 05, 2001). Temple Destruction and Indo-Muslim States, the Frontline, Pp. 70-77.

40   Ashraf, Ajaz (Nov 20, 2015). We will never know the number of temples desecrated through India's history': Richard Eaton, Interview, Scroll Online. https://scroll.in/article/769463/we-will-never-know-the-number-of-temples-desecrated-through-indias-history-richard-eaton Accessed October 26, 2023.

These historical perspectives are necessary to understand the events that gave birth to the oral narratives in this book. Every reasonable attempt has been made to stitch together and obtain the near-correct versions associated with each story concerning temples under discussion.

As mentioned earlier, the objective is to interrogate oral narratives concerning the temples through historical evidences, without apportioning praise or blame to actors on the scene at that time.

1
Vellayi and the Story of Sri Rangam

The Kakatiya dynasty at Warangal had reached great heights under its last ruler, Prataparudra (1290-1323 AD). In the year 1308, the Sultanate forces from Delhi led by Malik Kafur, the slave general of Allauddin Khilji, laid siege to Warangal fort resulting in the surrender of Prataparudra who furnished a large quantity of gold and valuables including the famous Koh-I-Noor diamond and agreed to pay an annual tribute to Delhi. Malik Kafur returned to Delhi with a booty of a hundred elephants, 7000 horses, and quantities of jewels[41]. However, he was not true to his word and Delhi forces returned to teach him a lesson in 1310. Having defeated him this time, Malik Kafur extracted a large tribute. By then, he had heard of untold riches held by temples in Malabar and Pandya kingdom of Madurai. Thus, he proceeded into Hoysala territory in Karnataka and further into Malabar. Hoysala king Veera Ballala III surrendered without much resistance in February 1311[42]. After extracting tributes, Malik Kafur proceeded to Pandya capital of Madurai. The pandya prince Sundara Pandya attempted to intercept Malik Kafur near Tichirappalli but was himself captured and executed. Malik Kafur's forces then looted the Sri Rangam and Chidambaram temples nearby.

The Bhattars (Acharya or priestly class) that look after the temple were initially confident that the Mohammedan forces would not reach Sri Rangam. However, when it was heard that Sundara Pandya was slain and Muslim forces have reached Samayapuram (about 12 km from Sri Rangam), they hastily planned to save the temple and its deities. Many sanctums of minor temples in the complex were hastily walled, the idol of the spiritual consort of Sri Ranganatha, Ranganayaki Thayar, was taken out and buried under a bhilva tree

---

41 Lane-Poole (1903). The Story of the nations: Mediaeval India under Mohammedan Rule 712-1764, New York: GP Putnam's Sons, p 114

42 Kamath S. U. (1980). A concise history of karnataka: From pre-historic times to the present. Bangalore: Archana Prakashana, p 129.

in the third prahara, and the main deity for daily worship (affectionately called Azhagiya Manavala) was entrusted to some priests to be hidden in the forests around Trichirapalli.

Even as these plans were in action, the Sultanate forces reached outer walls of the temple. Many residents of the seven prahara around the temple resisted the Sultanate forces but in vain. It was in those desperate moments that one of the devadasi[43] attached to the temple, Vellayi by name, came forward with a brilliant but eventually sad plan to keep the Muslim forces diverted so that the deity could be safely taken away.

Being well versed in classical dance and singing, Vellayi courted the Muslim chieftain who headed towards main sanctum. Attracted to her beauty, this chieftain halted the looting and followed her dancing and singing. Vellayi with her dancing skills led the chieftain away and up the 145 ft. tall eastern gopuram (the eastern tower) with a promise to reveal some loot. As they reached nearly the top of the gopuram, Vellayi pushed the chieftain causing him to fall to the ground and die. Anxious that she has affected a death, Vellayi also jumped from the gopuram and gave up her life.

Her actions bought the priests' time to have the golden deity moved away into the forest. However, unbeknown to them, Prataparudra forces who also assisted the Sultanate forces in Pandya territory were in the same forested area. They helped sultanate forces to confiscate and take the golden idol along with immense loot from the temple to Delhi. The loot from Dwarasamudra (Hoysala), Madurai and Sri Rangam were reported to be 'no less than 612 elephants, 20,000 horses, coffers of precious stones and pearls, and 96,000 mans of gold, which, taking the man at no more than\cwt., amounts to 1200 tons of gold'[44].

The sacrifice of Vellayi became a legend and survived through the calamitous times that followed the invasion by Sultanate forces. Seventy years later, a Vijayanagara Empire's chieftain would eventually force the eviction of Muslim forces that remained in control of the temple. He also commemorated the

---

43   In the temple traditions of ancient India, girls who wished to dedicate their life to the service of the temple were trained in various art forms like classical dance and instruments. They remained in the temple performing appropriate artistic rituals during the religious rites of the temple. They were known as 'devadasi' meaning the ritual servant of the Lord.

44   Lane-Poole (1903). The Story of the nations: Mediaeval India under Mohammedan Rule 712-1764, New York: GP Putnam's Sons, p 114

memory of Vellayi by having the eastern gopuram painted white. The gopuram came to be called Vellayi gopuram or Vellai gopuram as it is known today (Vellai in Tamil means white).

The golden idol taken away to Delhi survived mutilation or melting. It returned to Sri Rangam nearly seventy years later.

That story is narrated in the next chapter.

Vellayi Gopuram: Pic courtesy Wiki.

2
Pin Thodarntha Valli

Malik Kafur, the slave general of Allauddin Khilji, returned to Delhi with immense loot from Warangal, Dwarasamudra (named Halebedu now), Madurai, Sri Rangam and Chidambaram. The booty is said to have consisted of 'no less than 612 elephants, 20,000 horses, coffers of precious stones and pearls, and 96,000 mans of gold, which, taking the man at no more than\cwt., amounts to 1200 tons of gold'[45]. His campaign in the south commenced in October 1310 and ended in October 1311. He returned to Delhi with the treasures so obtained.

Allauddin Khilji was delighted to receive the booty and he ordered that it be proportionately distributed among the nobles, chieftains and the troops that participated in the raids. Apart from the booty, a large number of camp followers also had accompanied the forces who were absorbed in the capital into various households.

One amongst them was a young girl from Tiruvellarai[46] which is about 16 km from Sri Rangam. Being an ardent devotee of Sri Ranganatha and having heard of the sacking of Sri Rangam, she enrolled herself as a maid in the Sultanate forces in order to keep a track of the idol that was part of the loot taken to Delhi. At Delhi, when the loot was distributed to the nobles and chieftains, she gathered that the idol of Ranganatha (Utsava Murthi[47]) was given to a noble (Amir) at Khilji court by the name Abdullah Hussain Kasanbi Badshah[48].

---

45   Lane-Poole (1903). The Story of the nations: Mediaeval India under Mohammedan Rule 712-1764, New York: GP Putnam's Sons, p 114

46   Chockalingam (see the note below), however says that this girl was from Tirukkarambanur, a mere 3.5 km from the Sri Rangam temple across the Kollidam River. He also mentions that this girl visited the temple every day and would take her meal only after the darshan of Sri Ranganatha.

47   Utsava Murthi is the idol that is taken around the temple during ceremonial processions. It is made of either pure gold or panchaloka (combination of five metals).

48   Chockalingam, SP (2012). மதுரை சுல்தான்கள்: முகமதியர்களின் ஆட்சியில் தமிழகம். Chennai: கிழக்கு. p. 49.

The young girl managed to engage herself as a maid in the Amir's household and gained the confidence of his daughter Suradhani. In due course she discovered that the elegant Suradhani had indeed fallen in love with the idol of Ranganatha and kept it in her private quarters. To her surprise, she found that Suradhani was in fact so much in love with Sri Ranganatha that she talked to the idol, sang to it and appeared completely devoted to it.

After ascertaining all these, she managed to provide enough excuses so as to get leave granted from the Amir's house in the pretext of returning to Sri Rangam to visit her parents. She set course through the arduous country and eventually reached Sri Rangam. She provided necessary details to the acharyas and bhattars of the temple, assuring them the Lord was indeed kept in the personal protection of the princess in the Amir's household.

Excitement and anxiety together embarked upon the priests of the temple as well as devotees. The question in front was, how to retrieve Azhagiya Manavala back to Sri Rangam. After much deliberations, it was decided that a cultural troupe comprising of 50-60 artists will be sent under the leadership of the maid who knew the whereabouts of the utasava idol. Since this young girl of Tiruvellarai had taken exceptional risks to follow the Lord and find the exact location, she was bestowed the name 'Pin Thodarntha Valli' (the maiden who followed the Lord).

After necessary preparations, the troupe led by Pin Thodarntha Valli embarked upon the long and risky journey all the way to Delhi. Arriving safely and having been introduced to the Amir's court by her, they offered to entertain the Amir and his clan with their exceptional musical and dance talents. The Amir and Suradhani, happy to note the return of Pin Thodarntha Valli (as per her words), consented.

The scintillating performance by the troupe endeared them to the household and apparently they enjoyed immense hospitality in between their artistic displays. Having indulged in their art display and appreciative of their talents, Amir eventually asked them for whatever prize that would please them. Pin Thodarntha Valli and the troupe unanimously requested Amir to merely grant them the idol of Azhagiya Manavala, expressing their desire to continue to serve the Lord at Sri Rangam.

Touched by their piety, the Amir consented to have the idol given to them after his daughter Suradhani, who was in love with the same, goes to sleep. The Amir kept his word.

An exhilarated troupe, again led by Pin Thodarntha Valli, departed for Sri Rangam with the Lord's idol. However, when Suradhani woke up next day, she was dismayed at the developments and begged her father to send her to Sri Rangam to convince the troupe to return the idol to her. Suradhani and a troop of escorts thereafter departed for Sri Rangam.

In the meanwhile, fearing that the Muslim forces may intervene and snatch the idol away, Pin Thodarntha Valli and her group split up and went separate ways, distracting the pursuers. The group with the actual possession of the Lord made it across the Narmada and reached Tirupati, fearing that if they proceed to Sri Rangam the Lord may be snatched away. At Tirupati, the Lord was vested with a family of Kodava. The Kodava family retreated into the jungles and kept the Lord's idol safe apparently in caves.

In the meanwhile, Pin Thodarntha Valli and her companions continued to mislead the forces that were in pursuit and somewhere in this process of evading, lost their lives or at least no known record of them reaching back Sri Rangam exists.

The entertainment troupe who played key role in the retrieval of the idol from Delhi were bestowed with the name 'Isai Ariyum Perumal Koothaar' (The troupe of the Lord, who is the source of all music), a name that signifies the sacrifice they made in the service of the Lord by their musical talents.

As for Suradhani who followed the idol back to Sri Rangam, well, that is the next story.

3
Tulukka Nachiar

Sri Rangam temple located in a small island at the confluence of Kaveri River and Kollidam River near Tiruchirapalli was invaded at least thrice in the early years of 14th century. In 1311, Allauddin Khiliji's deputy Malik Kafur led the sacking of the town. It is during this invasion that Vellayi, the danseuse from the temple, bought time to save the looting of the utsava (deity of daily worship). Notwithstanding her sacrifice, the utsava idol (idol for daily worship) was taken away to Delhi. Her story is in the preceding pages.

After Pin Thodarntha Valli's heroic and successful attempt to bring the utsava idol, Suradhani the daughter of Amir Abdullah Hussain Kasanbi, followed the dance troupe of Pin Thodarntha Valli in the hope of retrieving the idol. Her pursuit however resulted in vain as the dance troupe, fearing reprisal by Muslim troops, spilt into two. They followed different and devious routes to evade capture.

One group with Pin Thodarntha Valli eventually disappeared in the vast country. There is no evidence at least till now as to the fate of the members of this group. Suradhani kept chasing them in vain and eventually reached Sri Rangam itself. The other group, fearing the capture and loss of the Lord, made its way to Tirupati. They confided in a Kodava family of the possibility of the pursuing forces finding the Lord and requested them to protect the same. The Kodava family took the Lord's idol into the deep jungles and kept it safe in caves.

In the meanwhile, Suradhani who reached the Sri Rangam temple did not find the idol there and in her exasperation fell at the entrance and gave up her life[49]. The archakas and bhattars of the temple were moved by the love she had for the Lord and in due course, her portrait inlaid in classical Tanjore style was installed in the North East corner of the 2nd prahara (circumambulation way)

---

49 Chockalingam, SP (2012). மதுரை சுல்தான்கள்: முகமதியர்களின் ஆட்சியில் தமிழகம். Chennai: கிழக்கு.

to commemorate her devotion. She was also deified with the name 'Tulukka Nachiar' meaning the Turkic consort of the Lord[50].

Suradhani with Azhagiya Manavala: Art by Deepak Saagar

⬅ Tulukka Nachiar

Kaili Tirumanjanam ➡

Source: https://kshetrapuranas.blogspot.com/2011/03/saga-of-thulukka-naachiyaar-sri-rangam.html

Even today, devotees visiting Sri Rangam pray at her shrine. To commemorate her eventual union with the Lord, on specified days a typical Muslim style roti

---

50 Davis, Richard H. (2004). "A Muslim princess in the temples of Viṣṇu". International Journal of Hindu Studies. Springer Nature. 8 (1–3): 137–156. doi:10.1007/s11407-004-0006-y

(leavened bread) and milk are offered to the Lord. On those days, the Lord is also adorned with a lungi in the style of a Mussalman, called in the typical Vaishnavite tradition as 'Kaili Tirumanjanam'. In colloquial Tamil, kaili means lungi. The Lord is also offered betel leaves with chuna (calcium hydroxide) applied on the front side, as per Muslim tradition.

4
The Story of Namperumal

It is curious but pertinent to note that many of the names by which Lord Ranganatha is affectionately and piously referred to are not derived only from scriptures or Divya Prabhanda[51] sung by His most ardent devotees, the Alvars[52]. They are also derived from tradition that deeply resonates with the devotion of all sections of the society towards the Lord, stepping beyond the perceived restrictions of caste. While Tulukka Nachiar epitomises the devotion of a Muslim princess, one such name 'Namperumal' affectionately used by the Vaishnavite across the world to refer to Lord Ranganatha came from a humble washer man.

We have read the stories of Pin Thodarntha Valli and Tulukka Nachiar in the previous pages. We also note that despite their valiant efforts, the idol of Azhagiya Manavala rested at Tirupati in the care and custody of a Kodava family. Chronologically, the arrival of the Lord's idol at Tirupati must have been in 1312 or 1313. It would reside there for nearly sixty years.

In the meanwhile, Sri Rangam was subjected to one more sacking by Muhammad bin Tughlaq, who succeeded Khilji dynasty in 1325 as sultan of Delhi. He was considered an eccentric and at times mad, so much so that scholars note him as 'The Eccentric Prince or The Mad Sultan'[53]. He was also known to have put to sword entire Hindu populations and was especially biased against the priestly class[54].

---

51   Divya Prabandha are the devotional hymns sung by Alvars.

52   Ardent devotees of Lord Vishnu who wrote volumes of devotional hymns are known as Alvar. The term literally means the one who is lorder by Vishnu. There are 12 Alvars viz., Poigai Alvar, Boothathu Alvar, Pei Alvar, Tirumazhisai Alvar, Nammalvar, Madhurakavi Alvar, Kulasekara Alvar, Periyalvar, Andal, Thondaradippodi Alvar, Tiruppan Alvar and Tirumangai Alvar. These Alvars lived in Tamil region between 6th and 9th century AD.

53   See: Douthwaite, John; Virdis, Daniela Francesca; Zurru, Elisabetta (2017). The Stylistics of Landscapes, the Landscapes of Stylistics. John Benjamins Publishing Company. p. 230. ISBN 978-90-272-6460-2.

54   Sewell, Robert. A Forgotten Empire (Vijayanagar). Swan Sonnenschein & Co. pp. 12–15.

The death of Allauddin Khilji in 1316 resulting in successive plots for succession by Malik Kafur and other Amirs had created political vacuum at Delhi. This enabled Ghyasuddin Tughlaq to ascend to power as founding sultan of Tughlaq dynasty in September 1320. Struggles for the throne of Delhi in the four years following Khilji's death provided ample room for Kakatiya ruler at Warangal, Prataparudra, to discontinue his tribute to Delhi court.

After ascending to throne of Delhi, Ghyasuddin Tughlaq despatched his young prince, Muhammad bin Tughlaq (also known as Prince Fakhr Malik Jauna Khan, Juna Khan or Ulugh Khan[55]) to Warangal to suppress Prataparudra. Descending through Yadava territory, ransacking Devagiri and extracting sumptuous tribute from Yadava, Muhammad Tughlaq arrived at Warangal in 1323. He was not successful in his initial attempt as Prataparudra had fortified Warangal and was prepared to withstand the siege. He even managed to take advantage of a confusion in the Tughlaq camp and successfully defeated him and drove him to Kotagiri[56] where another of Tughlaq commanders, Abu-Riza, was able to reinforce Tughlaq army. In the meanwhile, Prataparudra became complacent presuming retreat of Tughlaq as final defeat. He had even dispersed his army and the fort became vulnerable. Mohammed bin Tughlaq returned with reinforcements[57]. Unlike the earlier occasions when Prataparudra was allowed his life and kingdom in exchange for fealty and tribute to sultanate, this time he was defeated, imprisoned and escorted to Delhi[58]. Enroute to Delhi, Prataparudra died on the banks of Narmada River[59].

After despatching Prataparudra to Delhi, Muhammad bin Tughlaq continued his southern campaign. He went to Malabar and invested Kayalpatinam[60] from where he proceeded to Madurai and eventually turned up

---

55 Elliot and Dowson, Tárikh-i Fíroz Sháhí of Ziauddin Barani, The History of India, as Told by Its Own Historians. The Muhammadan Period (Vol 3), London, Trübner & Co

56 Kotagiri is a village in Nizamabad district in the state of Telangana in India. It is an ancient village ruled by kakatiyas near to bodhan.

57 Parabrahma Sastry, P. V. (1978). The Kākatiyas of Warangal. India: Government of Andhra Pradesh.

58 Sen, Sailendra (2013). A Textbook of Medieval Indian History. Primus Books. pp. 91–97. ISBN 978-9-38060-734-4.

59 Parabrahma Sastry, P. V. (1978). The Kākatiyas of Warangal. India: Government of Andhra Pradesh. Richard M. Eaton however believes that Prataparudra committed suicide to avoid imprisonment or ill-treatment at Delhi. See: Richard M. Eaton (2005). A Social History of the Deccan, 1300-1761. Cambridge University Press. ISBN 9780521254847.

60 Kayalpattinam is an ancient port city of the Pandya kingdom, also known as Korkau or Vaghuthai.

at Sri Rangam, having known of its immense riches brought to Delhi by Malik Kafur a decade earlier[61].

Despite the ravages experienced earlier, the devotees and priests of Sri Rangam put up a fierce resistance. It is said that over 13000 residents were put to sword and the city and temple were systematically looted[62]. Unlike Malik Kafur, Muhammad bin Tughlaq appointed Wazirs in the conquered territories and consolidated the expansion of his revenue network[63].

Amidst all these tumultuous events, the idol of Azhagiya Manavala continued to reside in the jungles around Tirupati with the Kodava custodians consciously watching the developments. The Lord continued to be in their custody.

In the year 1336, Vijayanagara was founded by five sons of Sangama of Warangal. Eldest among them, Harihara and his brother, Bukka had earlier served with Kakatiya king Prataparudra. They were part of the occurrences leading to the death of Prataparudra in 1323. When Warangal fell to Tughlaq forces, Harihara and Bukka found their way to Dwarasamudra of Hoysala in Karnataka and then to Anegundi where Vijayanagara was eventually established. The story of the founding of Vijayanagara will be visited later.

After Harihara, Bukka I (1343-1379)[64] ascended to power and extended the kingdom into Pandya territories. Sometime in 1375, his eldest son Kumara Kampana was despatched with an able general Gopanna to conquer Sambuvaraya of Kanchipuram. Though Sambuvaraya was defeated, Kanchipuram came directly under Vijayanagara only in 1382-83. Gopanna was appointed as the governor of Senji (this town is between Madras and Tiruvannamalai).

Marco Polo refers to Pazhaiyakayal (Old Payal), which is 15 km north of actual Kayalpatnam.

61   Chandra, Satish (1997). Medieval India: From Sultanate to the Mughals. New Delhi, India: Har-Anand Publications. pp. 101–102. ISBN 978-8124105221.

62   Historians and chroniclers often mention that Ulugh Khan of the Allauddin Khilji's time or Malik kafur (Khilji's slave general) looted Sri Rangam in 1323. These inferences are misplaced. Allauddin Khilji's brother Almas Beg was also known as Ulugh Khan. This Ulugh Khan was governor of Malwa. He never raided southern India. See: Banarsi Prasad Saksena (1992). *The Khaljis: Alauddin Khalji*. In Mohammad Habib and Khaliq Ahmad Nizami (ed.). A Comprehensive History of India: The Delhi Sultanat (A.D. 1206–1526). Vol. 5 (Second ed.) The Indian History Congress / People's Publishing House & Khan, AD (2021). A History of the Sadarat in Medieval India Volume- I (Pre-Mughal Period). Chennai: K.K. Publications, p 150.

Muhammed bin Tughlaq was also known as Ulugh Khan. See: Khan, AD (2021). A History of the Sadarat in Medieval India Volume- I (Pre-Mughal Period). Chennai: K.K. Publications

63   ibid

64   Sewell, Robert, The Forgotten Empire, p 46

Gopanna is said to be of Brahmin birth and an ardent devotee of Lord Venkateswara of Tirupati. During one of his visits, he discovered that idol of Azhagiya Manavala was at Tirupati. Convincing the Kodava clan and priests of Tirupati, Gopanna brought Azhagiya Manavala to Senji, had a cave temple constructed and installed the idol till a suitable time arrived to have the idol restored to Sri Rangam[65].

In the meanwhile, at Sri Rangam the Muslim governor (appointed by Muhammad bin Tughlaq) who had initially stayed in the temple premises itself, moved to Samayapuram and constructed a small fortress for himself with the stones of the demolished prahara (circumambulation path) of the temple. A dancing girl (devadasi) from the temple who attracted the Muslim governor's attention had also moved to Samayapuram with him. She inducted a Kaniyala-brahmin by name Singappiran into services of the governor. Between the two, they kept an eye on all activities of Mussalman forces and prevented further damages to temple. When Singappiran came to know of the establishment of Gopanna at Senji, his son Tirumanattu-nambi arranged for a sthallatar (temple administrator) by name Uttama-nambi to travel to Senji and appraise Gopanna of the events at Sri Rangam. Ten years would further pass before Tirumanattu-nambi finally sent word to Gopanna that the time was ripe and Muslim governor had let all caution into the air, drowned as he was in the pleasures of women[66].

Gopanna proceeded to Sri Rangam and vanquished the Muslim governor in 1393. Sri Rangam was restored and all ravages caused by invaders were repaired and restored. It is during this time, that Gopanna heard of the sacrifice of Vellayi during the invasion by Malik Kafur in 1310. In her memory, he had the eastern tower (gopuram) painted white.

He also brought the idol of Azhagiya Manavala from Senji to be installed in the main temple.

In the intervening seven decades, the priests at Sri Rangam continued their worship, having lost their heart on the recovery of original idol of Azhagiya Manavala after Tulukka Nachiar incident. Composing themselves, they had installed a panchaloka (made of five metals) idol of the Lord in place of the original. This panchaloka idol was in worship for over 70 years, when Gopanna returned victoriously with original idol of Azhagiya Manavala from Senji.

---

65 Sastri, Harihara G. & Sastri, Srinivasa V. (Eds.) (1924). Madhura Vijaya or Virakamparaya Charita: A Historical Kavya by Gangadevi, Trivandrum: Srihara Power Press, pp 12-13.

66 Ibid, Pp 13-14.

The Story of Namperumal

Doubts and anxiety prevailed in the temple town since Gopanna had restored their honour by saving the town, but the veracity of Senji idol dogged them. They somehow convinced Gopanna to have the idol kept in the 3rd prahara till an answer to their anxiety was found.

The answer came in the form of a dream to a bhattar of the temple. The Lord appeared to him in the dream stating that he would not enter the sanctum unless accompanied by his consort, Ranganayaki Thayar. In the same time, in another dream, Ranganayaki Thayar appeared in front of a 13 year old girl, directing her to dig under the Bhilva tree in the 3rd prahara.

The puzzled girl and Bhattar proceeded to the 3rd prahara and began digging below the tree. The idol of Ranganayaki Thayar buried by one of the devotees in 1310 under that tree was found.

Excitement electrified Sri Rangam. The coincidence of Senji idol stopping in 3rd prahara, the dreams and discovery of idol of Ranganayaki Thayar was not missed. Curiously, it still did not convince the bhattars of the temple to have the Senji idol installed back. After prolonged deliberations, temple priests began to look for someone who had lived during the events of 1310 in order to validate or obtain some clarity. They eventually found a septa/octogenarian washer man whose task it was to wash the cloth that adorned the idol of Lord Ranganatha. Things become more complex when they discovered that the old washer man was also blind.

The blind washer man however was of an alert mind and he offered a solution: he had the good fortune of partaking the tirumanjana theertham[67] from the cloth of the Lord every day since his childhood. His father used to wring the cloth and advise him to imbibe the same before washing. He told the priests that having imbibed the holy water for years, he can discern the theertham from the original idol.

Relieved at the solution arrived at, tirumanjana abhishekam (holy bath) was performed on the idol brought from Senji. To every one's surprise and delight, when the blind washer man took it, he excitedly called out 'this indeed is our Lord' in Tamil using the term 'Nam Perumal' (our Lord). An electric excitement bordering on the eccentric cruised through Sri Rangam. The Lord had indeed

---

67 Holy water dripping from the clothe after the Lord was bathed. This is considered as a heavenly blessing among Hindu devotees, irrespective of the god they worship. Tirumanjanam means bathing of the Lord, an expression specifically used by Iyengars of Tamil country.

returned home together with his spiritual consort![68]

Vedanta Desika who had exiled himself to Sathyamangalam during these events, returned to Sri Rangam to witness the events. Stepping beyond his exclusive devotion to the Lord, he even composed two sloka praising Gopanna for his exceptional service, a matter that is unique in bhakti traditions where a 'nara' (human being) was praised by a most ardent devotee of the Lord. This 'Nara Stuti' (praise to a human being) is recorded in an inscription on the eastern wall of the 1st prahara (Prakara-the circumambulatory path).

The washer man was immortalized by a title Eeram Kolli of the temple. (The recognizer of wetness), to commemorate his exceptional service in identifying the Lord.

Namperumal then was installed in the garbhagriha accompanied by Ranganayaki Thayar with much fanfare and rituals. Even today, when we visit Sri Rangam, we find two utsava idols in the sanctum sanctorum!

Namperumal

---

68 Dr. S Krishnaswami Iyengar, one of the foremost scholars on the events of this time, places the period of these occurrences between 1343 and 1356 based on an examination of the coinage of the Madurai Sultans and archaeological evidences concerning them. They do prove that the interpretation of GH Sastri & VS Sastri in Madura Vijaya by Gangadevi, queen of Kumara kampana.

The Story of Namperumal

स्वांत श्रीः बन्धुप्रिये शकाब्दे (शकाब्द १२०३)

1. आनीयानीलशृङ्गद्युतिरचितजगद्रञ्जनादञ्जनाद्रे:
चेञ्चुधामाराध्य कञ्चित्समयमथ निहत्योद्धनुष्कान् तुलुष्कान् ।
लक्ष्मीक्ष्माभ्यामुभाभ्यां सह निजनगरे स्थापयन् रङ्गनाथं
सम्यग्वर्यां सपर्यां पुनरकृत यशोदर्पणो गोप्पणार्यः ॥

2. विश्वेशं रङ्गराजं वृषभगिरितटाद् गोप्पणक्षोणिदेवो
नीत्वा स्वां राजधानीं निजबलनिहतोत्सिक्ततौलुष्कसैन्यः ।
कृत्वा श्रीरङ्गभूमिं कृतयुगसहितां तं च लक्ष्मीमहीभ्यां
संस्थाप्यास्यां सरोजोद्भव इव कुरुते साधुचर्यासपर्याम् ॥

(After bringing Sri Ranganatha from Anjanadri (Tirumalai), which delights the world with its peaks covered with dark clouds, and worshipping Him for some time at Chenchi with Sri Devi and Bhu Devi, Goppanarya, who is like a mirror of fame, vanquished the Muhammadans, who were expert archers, and re-installing the Lord at His own city of Srirangam, restored the traditional system of worship in the temple.

Goppanarya, the Brahmin, brought Sri Rangaraja, the Lord of the Universe, from the slope of the Vrishabhagiri (Tirumalai) to his capital and after destroying the Muslim army with his forces, reinstalled Him with Sri and Bhumi at Srirangam and thus introduced the Krita Yuga there again. In this deed, which is praised by all righteous men, he acted like the very Brahma, (the Lotus-Born).*

Source: Koil Ozughu, Pp 57-58.

5
Ramanuja and Bibi Nachiar

Sriman Ramanujacharya is the founder of Visishtadvaita School of philosophy. Apart from Adi Shankara who founded the Advaita and Madhvacharya who founded the Dvaita schools of philosophy, Ramanujacharya is the third saint who is instrumental in consolidating the philosophical foundations of Hindu belief. He is also celebrated as a secular idol for he admitted all castes into worship of the Lord, ordaining even untouchable sections of society as priests. Sri Vaishnava as they are known, are staunch adherents of vaishanvism and worship Lord Ranganatha of Sri Rangam as their prime deity.

Ramanuja was born in 1017 at Sriperumpudur in the outskirts of Chennai and went to Kanchipuram where he enrolled as a student of Yadava Prakasa. Yadava Prakasa was a staunch advocate of Dualism (Advaita). The student in this case is said to have converted the teacher to a new school of philosophy[69], Visishtatdvaita that believed in bhakti as a bridge to elevate the devotee to abode of the Lord. Ramanuja married and led a life of a priest in Varadaraja Perumal temple at Kanchipuram.

Yamunacharya who was the religious head of Sri Rangam temple had heard of the philosophical explorations of Ramanuja and caused his disciple, Sri Mahapurna to fetch Ramanuja to Sri Rangam in order to pass on affairs of the temple to him. Thus Ramanuja arrived at Sri Rangam only to discover that Yamunacharya had in the meantime passed away. A heartbroken Ramanuja returned to Kanchipuram believing that it was Sri Ranganatha's desire not to have him at Sri Rangam. However, destiny in the form of another great scholar, Kanchipurna, would cause him to proceed to Sri Rangam and serve Sri Ranganatha along with Yamunacharya's son, Tiruvaranga Araiyar and Sri Mahapurna. He is credited to have organized and systematised Sri Vaishhnava

---

69 Olivelle, Patrick (1992). The Samnyasa Upanisads: Hindu Scriptures on Asceticism and Renunciation: Hindu Scriptures on Asceticism and Renunciation. Oxford University Press. pp. 10–11, 17–18. ISBN 978-0-19-536137-7.

traditions of worship that are followed ever since by Sri Vaishnava community.

This was the time when Kirumikanta Chola (also known as Adirajendira) ascended to Chola throne with the help of Vikramaditya at Kanchipuram. He ruled from 1133 to 1150. He was an ardent devotee of Siva so much so that he even shifted his capital from Gangaikonda Cholapuram to Chidambaram where the famous Nataraja temple is located. Holding Siva as the only god, the Chola king persecuted Vaishnavas and caused immeasurable damages to Vishnu temples. His oppression against Vaishnavas resulted in Ramanuja proceeding to Hoysala kingdom ruled by Bitti Deva, a king who followed Jainism but tolerant towards others.

Ramanuja met Bitti Deva and was able to bring him back to Vaishnava faith with the new title, Vishnuvardhana I[70] [71] (1018-1152). This king built the Tirunarayanaswamy temple at Melukote (Mandya district of Karnataka), Keerthi Narayana temple at Talakad, and the spectacular Vijayanarayana temple at Belur (known as the Chennakesava Temple, dedicated to Vishnu). Ramanuja stayed in Hoysala territory for about 14 years[72]. In the interim, Adirajendra had died during a religious uprising in Chola country due to his intolerance towards Vaishnavaites[73].

It is during his stay at Tirunarayanapuram (Melukote owing to the Tirunarayanaswamy temple there), that Ramanuja came to know that an idol of the Lord at Yadavadri had earlier been taken by an invading Muslim king to Delhi[74].

Ramanuja's arrival at Tirunarayanapuram (Melukote) itself is an interesting story, as narrated in Ramanuja Digvijayam by APN Swami[75]. When Ramanuja commenced his journey to Hoysala territory, he carried with him white tiruman (holy sand dust of white colour which the Vaishnava wear on their forehead). However, as he proceeded through jungles and country side, halting at

---

70 Smith, Vincent Aurthur (1920), The Oxford History of India: From the Earliest Times to the End of 1911, Clarendon Press

71 Govindāchārya, Alkandavilli (1906), The life of Ramanujacharya: the exponent of the Visistadvaita philosophy, Madras: S. Murthy and Co.

72 Kamath, Suryanath U. (2001) [1980], A concise history of Karnataka: from pre-historic times to the present, Bangalore: Jupiter books,

73 Sastri, KAN (1975). A History of South India: From Prehistoric Times to the Fall of Vijayanagara, New Delhi: Oxford University Press, 4th Edition, 51st Impression, Pp 171-172.

74 Parthasarathy, TS (1954). The Koil Ozhugu, Tirupati: Tirumala Tirupati Devasthanam, Pp 39-40.

75 Swami, APN (2018). Ramanuja Digvijayam (English version), Chennai: Panchjanyam Trust, Pp 27-33.

Tirumaliruncholai and other places, his stock of tiruman was depleting. When he met Bitti Deva and successfully brought him into Vaishnava faith, Ramanuja expressed his desire to obtain tiruman wherever it could be found.

The king indicated that there was a temple somewhere in a hilly area that was dedicated to Lord Narayana, stating with a deep sense of regret that he had failed to maintain it owing to his Jain belief earlier. That night, Ramanuja had a dream in which Lord Narayana appeared and guided him as to the path to the erstwhile temple area. On the following day, Ramanuja followed by the king reached the place by the side of a pond, among hills and found a huge ant hill made of same tiruman that he was in search of. This pond is now called Kalyani pushkarani.

The king caused a huge quantity of milk to be poured on the ant hill in order to have it made into paste. To the delight of Ramanuja, the derided ant hill revealed an exceptionally well made statute of Lord Narayana with goddess Lakshmi seated at his feet. Ramanuja retrieved the idol and king Vishnuvardhana built a temple for the Lord under Ramanuja's supervision. This became the Cheluva Narayanaswamy temple at Melukote that we get to visit today.

Melukote Kalyani Pushkarani

Cheluva Narayanaswamy Temple, Melukote. Pic courtesy: Wiki

Cheluva Narayanaswamy with Mahalakshmi seated at his holy feet. Pic courtesy: Wiki

The construction of this temple probably was in about 1098 since at least one source mentions that Ramanuja worshipped here in December 1098. The source citing the report of Mysore Archaeological Department says[76]:

> *According to a legend, this metallic image was lost for many centuries and was recovered by Sri Ramanujacharya. The annual report of the Mysore Archaeological Department (p. 57) states, on the strength of epigraphic evidence, that the presiding deity of this temple was already a well-known object of worship before Sri Ramanujacharya worshipped at the shrine, in December 1098, and even before he came to the Mysore region.*

Ramanuja Digvijayam however goes on to say that Sri Ramanuja was told that the idol (affectionately called Sri Ramapriya[77]) was taken to Delhi during the raids of Mussalman armies from the north. It narrates the story as below[78]:

> *Learning that the idol has been taken to Delhi, Ramanuja determined to travel to the palace of the sultan and have the idol returned. He was followed by a large group of disciples.*
>
> *The sultan at Delhi received him with great respect and even agreed to return the idol, asking Ramanuja himself to take it from the treasury. However the idol was not found in the treasury and therefore Ramanuja prayed to the Lord to reveal himself.*
>
> *The Lord then guided Ramanuja to go to the harem of the sultan and sing his praise. Ramanuja, accompanied by the sultan proceeded to the harem where he sang Tamil couplets affectionately calling the Lord 'Chella Pillai' (dear child). The intense verses sung by Ramanuja resulted in the deity that was kept in the chamber of the princess to 'walk' to Ramanuja. Thoroughly*

---

76 https://en.wikipedia.org/wiki/Melukote

77 The idol of Cheluva Narayanaswamy is also fondly referred to as Ramapriya. Epic and mythological legends say that this Lord was worshipped by Sri Ram. It is said to have been revealed or given to Lord Krishna by Sri Ram himself. During the course of the visit of Balarama (brother of Sri Krishna) to Narayanadri (the hill on which the temple is located now), he is said to have found only the main deity and asked Krishna to bring the idol of Ramapriya to Narayanadri and install it as utsava idol. Since Sri Krishna installed the idol here There are two temples for Sri Rama at Melukote. Sri Rama Devura Gudi that is about 800 m and Sri Pattabhi Rama temple that is about 150 m, from Cheluva Narayanaswamy temple respectively.

78 Swami, APN (2018). Ramanuja Digvijayam (English version), Chennai: Panchjanyam Trust, Pp. 30-48.

impressed by the piety of Ramanuja, the sultan permitted him to carry the idol back.

The princess who was in deep love with the Lord pleaded with Ramanuja and the sultan to allow her to accompany the Lord back to Tirunarayanapuram. Enroute south, as the legend says, the princess disappeared from her palanquin. Ramanuja then discerned that she had merged with the Lord through her bhakti and had her immortalized by calling her 'Bibi Nachiar' (the Muslim consort of Sri Narayana).

Note: *This story is also found in a different version at a blog https://kshetrapuranas.wordpress.com/2009/03/09/thulukka-naachiyaar-the-melkote-version/ that appears to have been taken from Ramanuja Digvijayam. Many other travelogues and blogs tend to present their own versions, essentially drawing from other blogs/websites carrying similar versions.*

A Historical Review

While the legend stated in Ramanuja Digvijayam is worthy of veneration owing to the cult of bhakti that it promotes, historical evidence suggests that the story of Bibi Nachiar of Melukote is by conjecture drawn from Tulukka Nachiar story that we visited earlier. To appreciate its historical significance, a brief discussion here is appropriate.

Historians of India including KA Neelakanta Sastri and AL Basham as well as the exceptionally collected seven volume 'Cultural Heritage of India' published by Ramakrishna Mission under the editorship of Sarvepalli Radhakrishnan, agree that the Muslim inroads in the north west of India occurred first with the advent of Ghori. The house of Ghurids ruled from 7th century till 1215 AD.

From historical records, we find the genealogy of Ghurids[79][80] as under:

---

[79] Department of Islamic Art. "List of Sultanate and Mughal Dynastic Rulers of South Asia." In Heilbrunn Timeline of Art History. New York: The Metropolitan Museum of Art, 2000–. http://www.metmuseum.org/toah/hd/ssar/hd_ssar.htm (October 2004)

[80] Bosworth, C. Edmund (2001b). "Ghurids". Encyclopædia Iranica, online edition, Vol. X, Fasc. 6. New York. pp. 586–590.

Sultan	Period AD
Muhammad	632-661
Abu Ali Mohammad	1011-1035
Abbas ibn Shith	1035 – 1060
Qutb al-din Hasan	1080 – 1100
Izz al-Din Husayn	1100–1146
Sayf al-Din Suri	1146–1149
Baha al-Din Sam I	1149
Ala al-Din Husayn	1149–1161
Sayf al-Din Muhammad	1161–1163
Ghiyath al-Din Muhammad	1163–1203

Amongst these, Abu Ali Mohammad, Abbas ibn Shith, Qutb al-din Hasan, and Izz al-din Husayn Sayf al-Din Suri are the closest contemporaries to Ramanuja. Abu Ali Mohammad in fact was a pagan, who later converted to Islam[81]. All these Ghurid rulers were limited to Ghor and their kingdom did not expand into Indian subcontinent. In any case, they never descended below Punjab.

Muhammad of Ghor or Muhammad Ghori as he is known in India (Mu'izz ad-Din Muhammad ibn Sam, 1144-1206) is the other ruler from Ghori clan who made multiple raids into Hindustan. He raided Punjab, Gujarat and upto Mount Abu in Rajasthan today. He defeated Prithviraj Chauhan finally in the 2nd battle of Tarain in 1192 and installed Qutb Uddin Aibak as the governor of Delhi in 1192-1193. This period falls almost six decades after the life of Ramanuja and therefore even a conjuncture that Ramanuja visited Delhi during this time is not supported by historical evidence.

The other dynasty, Ghaznavid from Ghaznavi, was in permanent conflict with Ghurids and in due course became vassals of Ghurid. The most famous among them, Yamīn-ud-Dawla Abul-Qāsim Maḥmūd ibn Sebüktegīn or Mahmud of Ghazni (971-1030) as he is known in India, ruled from Ghaznavi

---

81 Ibid

but did not create a vassal ruler in Delhi. While Ghazni's sacking of Somnath[82] (1025) and Mathura[83] (Brindavan) in 1018-1020[84] is part of Indian lore, his expeditions appear to be limited to the temples north of Narmada River. No historical evidence is available to show that he could have reached Hoysala territory and looted a temple at Melukote. Considering that he died in 1030, and Ramanuja reached Melukote about seven decades later, it is not imaginable that a legend surrounding Muslim invasion was narrated to him six decades later. Vishnuvardhana, the king who ruled that area from 1108 in any case does not appear to be so informed. This historical construction in fact puts into question the discovery of Cheluva Narayana temple or the construction of it in 1098 itself, as stated in the Wiki source citing Annual Report of the Mysore Archaeological Department.

Enquiring further into the historical events of that time, we find five important personages who could have had the sway over Delhi. They are:

Ghazi Salar Masud or **Ghazi Miyan** (1014 – 1034 CE). Driven by martial and religious fervour, Salar Masud asked the Ghaznavid emperor to be allowed to march to India and spread his empire and Islam there. At the age of 16, he invaded India, crossing the Indus River. He conquered Multan, and after 18 months of campaign, he arrived near Delhi. With help of a reinforcement from Ghazni, he conquered Delhi and remained there for 6 months. He then conquered Meerut after some resistance. Next, he proceeded to Kannauj, whose ruler received him as friend[85]. Salar Masud was known for looting Hindu shrines and breaking idols. He considered it as his sacred duty. He is reported to have advised Mahmud of Ghazni to desecrate and break the idol of Somnath, when Mahmud actually hesitated to do so[86]. He attacked, looted and vandalized Mathura, as recorded by HM Elliot and John Dawson:

> *He first came to Mathura, and plundered that nest of idolatry which was a very holy spot among the people of India. After subduing and*

---

82   Thapar, Romila (2005). Somanatha: The Many Voices of a History. Penguin Books India. ISBN 9781844670208.

83   Grousset, René (1970). The Empire of the Steppes: A History of Central Asia. Rutgers University Press

84   Barua, Pradeep P. (2005). The State at War in South Asia. University of Nebraska Press.

85   Benett, WC (1877). Gazetteer of the province of Oudh. Vol. 2. North-Western Provinces and Oudh Government Press. Also see: https://en.wikiquote.org/wiki/Ghazi_Saiyyad_Salar_Masud

86   Elliot, HM & Dawson, John (1869). History of India as told by its own historians, Vol. II, London: Trubner & Co, p. 524-547

plundering all the chiefs of the neighbourhood who were reported to the rebellious and factious, he next proceeded against Kai Ajipal, the King of Kanauj, who did not venture to resist him, but fled...(p 519).

Ibrahim of Ghazna (b. 1033 – d. 1099). He had led many successful raids into the Gangetic plains and Rajasthan from 1063 to 1079. His commander Abdul Najam Zarir Shaybani carried the attacks to Varanasi, Thanesar and Kannauj. He however did not occupy any throne in Delhi and his Abdul Najam Zarir Shaybani was the military commander of Lahore, after Ibrahim captured it in August 1079[87]. He had just one son, Masud III.

Mas'ūd III of Ghazna (b. 1061 – d. 1115) had three sons by the name Shir-Zad of Ghazna, Arslan-Shah of Ghazna and Bahram-Shah of Ghazna. Masud was the brother of Ibrahim of Ghazna (1033-1099) who had appointed Masud III as his governor of Indian territories[88]. He became the sultan after his brother died and ruled for 16 years from 1099 to 1115. Historical records do not reveal him as occupying Delhi or as having any daughter.

Prithvirāja I (r. c. 1090-1110 CE). The Chahamana king who ruled during 1090 to 1110 was a staunch Shaivaite. However, he also liberally donated to other shrines, including that of Jains. The *Prabandha Kosha* states that Prithviraja 'pulled away the arms of one Baguli Shah[89], apparently referring to the repulsion of a Ghaznavid invasion. Minhaj-i-Siraj, in his *Tabaqat-i Nasiri*, mentions that during the reign of Mas'ud III, the Ghaznavid general Hajib Taghatigin raided India, going beyond the Ganga River, looting and destroying temples. It is possible that Baguli Shah was a subordinate of Hajib Taghatigin[90].

Ajayaraja II (r. c. 1110–1135 CE) of the Chahamaha dynasty established the city of Ajmer, and defeated Ghaznavids. It is during his time that Bharam Shah made several raids into India. Ajayaraja's silver coins have been found at many places, including Rajasthan and Mathura. These coins feature a seated goddess on one side, and the legend "Shri Ajayadeva" on the other side[91].

The examination of the campaigns and events concerning the five rulers/

---

87 Bosworth, C.E. (1977). The Later Ghaznavids. Columbia University Press
88 Ibid.
89 Singh, RB. (1964). *History of the chahamānas* (1st ed.), Varanasi: N. Kishore, Pp 128-129.
90 Nevill, HR (1905). Fyzabad: A Gazetteer, Vol. XLIII, Allahabad: Govet. Press United Province, p 150.
91 Singh, RB (1964). History of the Chahamanas (1st ed.), Varanasi: N. Kishore, p 132.

invaders (who could be contemporaries of Ramanuja) also bring out that Mathura was subjected to either protection by the Chahamana kings or looting and destruction by Ghaznavids and their generals, whether such invading forces occupied Delhi or not. Amongst these rulers, Prithviraja I and his son Ajayaraja II perhaps answer the part in Ramanuja's sojourn to the north for the idol of Ramapriya.

Considering that Lord Krishna's life, in lore or otherwise, is inextricably linked with Mathura, it may be safe to presume (however indulgent that presumption be!) that the idol of Ramapriya remained at Mathura or in the control of Prithviraja I or Ajayaraja II who also appear to have ruled that area during the life of Ramanuja at Melukote. Given this case, it would be eminently possible for him to obtain it from the king and bring it back to Melukote. The other three Muslim rulers, as recorded in history, are reputed to be destroyers of idols and at least two of them had vandalized and destroyed Mathura. Thus, they or their commanders having allowed Ramanuja to obtain the idol from them appears to be a historical impossibility.

A second presumption that could be safely arrived about the idol of Ramapriya rests on the Mysore Archaeological report mentioned earlier. As per the report, 'the metallic idol was obtained by Ramanuja from the lake (Kalyani Pushkarani). This appears more probable.

One question still remains: What is the story of Bibi Nachiar at Melukote?

For the time being, these historical factors would surmise that Ramanujacharya's life at Melukote is fully supported by valid sources while the story relating to Bibi Nachiar appears to be a later addition. This is possible considering the story of Tulukka Nachiar at Sri Rangam for which some supporting evidences are available in historical records.

It is to be recognized that bhakti (devotion) is not dependent on history. It may in fact create a history of its own, as witnessed in all civilizations across the world where legends of great saints and devotees sometimes do sit at variance with historical records. To presume that being scientific in our approach means being dependent on physical evidences alone to arrive at conclusions is rather inappropriate. We must recognize that science as we call it, has reached only a certain level of confidence in discerning things since the tools of modern science (obviously in a western connotation) are only five or six centuries old. Evolution of human and civilizational life dates many millennia before.

We do not need a lengthy discourse to appreciate that the great Rajaraja I (947-1014) who built Brihadeeswara temple at Thanjavore (Tanjore) had a highly evolved architectural science available to him. Brihadeeswaram could not have been built otherwise. Some 1300 years before him, the Saluvankuppam Murugan Temple was built!![92] Thus, if we remove the constriction that all our present and past knowledge is to be viewed from within the confines of modern science of the west, we will discover that there is an universe to be discovered in what AL Basham famously called 'A Wonder that was India'.

---

92   Subramanian, N. (21 September 2005). 'Remains of ancient temple found'. The Hindu. See also: https://web.archive.org/web/20120915014729/http://articles.timesofindia.indiatimes.com/2010-08-01/chennai/28281794_1_inscription-shore-temple-oldest-temples

6
Malik Kafur and the Looting of Madurai

Malik Kafur, the slave general of Allauddin Khilji, arrived at the gates of Madurai sometime in early April 1311[93]. Ruler of the Pandya kingdom, Veera Pandya and his brother Sundara Pandya had a bitter feud over the throne at Madurai and historians note that this feud was availed as an opportunity by Malik Kafur to raid Madurai. In any case, during his raid on Ballala king of Hoysala, he had ample hints about rich temples in Pandya kingdom.

The story as retold in popular Media

Malik Kafur had proceeded from Dwarasamudra of Hoysala country and was reaching for Madurai when Sundara Pandya set out to meet the invaders near Tiruchirapalli. Leaving Madurai in the care of Veera Pandya, Sundara had set course with a considerable army and reached the whereabouts of Melai Tirukkattupalli near Trichirapalli. Unfortunately for him, in the scorching summer of 1311, Cauvery River had practically run dry and his troops and horses were said to have been famished. He was also let down by a troop of 20000 Muslim cavalry in his service, who now willingly changed over to Malik Kafur's side. The battle with Malik Kafur's forces resulted in a route. Sundara Pandya was captured and beheaded by Malik Kafur.

Unopposed, Kafur looted the temples of Sri Rangam and Chidambaram and then proceeded to attack Madurai. Fearing Muslim onslaught, an uncle of Veera Pandya led a strong force to delay the arrival of Malik Kafur and to provide time for Veera Pandya to escape from Madurai. The uncle's forces where overwhelmed, though it is noted that they fought valiantly. Malik Kafur eventually reached the gates of Madurai on 24 April 1311.

---

93 Tara Boland-Crewe and David Lea note this as sometime in 1310. See: Tara Boland-Crewe; David Lea (2003). The Territories and States of India. London: Routledge. p. 401. ISBN 978-1-135-35624-8

Having heard of the looting and desecration at Sri Rangam and Chidambaram, priests of Madurai Meenakshi led by Sivachariars (the spiritual leaders of Siva worshippers) decided to save the main deity from desecration. They constructed a stone wall in front of garbhagriha (sanctum sanctorum) and installed a stone deity in front, imitating the now hidden sanctum. Despite conciliations and huge loot accumulated from the city, Malik Kafur proceeded to destroy the temple. The dummy garbhagriha was also damaged. The linga (phallic image of Lord Shiva) was broken and all the valuables were taken away. Fearing complete destruction of the temple town, Veera Pandya had it conveyed to Malik Kafur that a large ransom would be paid if further destruction was spared.

A colossal 96000 gold coins, half of elephants and horses and other valuable jewellery were taken as ransom. A Muslim governor was left in Madurai and Malik Kafur returned to Delhi with the combined loot of the temples and treasuries of South India. The Pandya kingdom effectively ceased to exist and survived as a minor vassal till Vijayanagara Empire rose to restore the temple and the former glory of Madurai.

KA Nilakanta Sastri's version:

Nilakanta Sastri states that both the Pandya princes were involved in an internal feud but they united against the invading forces of Malik Kafur. Veera Pandya at that time ruled from Bir Dhul (Viradhavalapattanam[94]) situated near Kanchipuram. Realising that Muslim forces specialized in siege techniques, Veera Pandya left his fortress at Bir Dhul and escaped by constantly harassing invading forces in the country side. However, Malik Kafur was successful in looting Kanchipuram and even destroying its biggest temple. He also managed to capture the treasure of Veera Pandya that was mounted on 120 elephants, near Kandur. But Veera Pandya escaped capture. Malik Kafur then turned his attention on Madurai itself where Sundara Pandya was king. Being forewarned, Sundara Pandya despatched his uncle, Vikrama Pandya, with a sizeable force. The forces of Delhi were successfully routed and Malik Kafur was forced to return to Delhi with the huge loot he had obtained, but without capturing Madurai[95] [96].

---

94 Sastri, KAN (1975). A History of South India: From Prehistoric Times to the fall of Vijayanagara, New Delhi: Oxford University Press, p 210.

95 Ibid, p 208-209.

96 George Michell however incorrectly notes that malik Kafur occupied Madurai in 1323. Malik Kafur

The question of Malik Kafur vandalizing Chidambaram or Madurai Meenakshi temple as recounted in oral traditions does not find support in historical sources. Zia Uddin Barani of those times records it in his Tarikh-i-Shahi[97] in the following words:

> *In their determination to secure whatever treasures might have been hidden away the invaders are said to have pulled down the temple's walls and dug up its foundations: 'Wherever there was any treasure in that deserted building, the ground was sifted in a sieve and the treasure discovered.' Malik Kafur then moved on to Madurai, where he stripped the famous temple of Meenakshi Amman of its golden roof and the golden image of the goddess. 'He destroyed the golden idol temple of Ma'bar,' wrote Malik Kafur's contemporary, the historian Zia-ud-Din Barani, 'and the golden idols which for centuries had been worshipped by the Hindus of that country. The fragments of the golden temple, and the broken idols of gold and gilt became the rich spoils of the army.'*

However, Barani's version appears to be an exaggeration. Francis Buchanan Hamilton[98] who travelled in these parts extensively in 1807 notes:

> *It has been pointed out to me that both here at Chidambaram and at Madurai the temple structures, much of which pre-date these raids, show no signs of extensive damage. So a case of hyperbole or just good restoration?*

Charles Allen who was familiar with the history of Muslim invasions, also travelled extensively through Coramandal and noted the following in his book:

> *From time to time tangible evidence of Ala-ud-Din's impact on the South continues to come to light as farmers and construction workers stumble upon carefully buried temple deities, as happened in August 1987 when workmen renovating the temple of Tiruramanathesvara in Esalam village in South Arcot District, inland from Pondicherry, came across four layers of buried*

---

was murdered at Delhi in 1316, after his machinations to remove the Khilji clan from the throne were discovered and disliked by the nobles of the court. See: Michell, George (1995), Architecture and art of southern India: Vijayanagara and, Volume 1, Issue 6, New York: Cambridge University Press, ISBN 978-0-521-44110-0, p. 9.

97 Zia-ud-Din Barni, Tarikh-i Shahi, tr. Sir H. H. Elliot and John Downson, The history of India, as told by its own historians, Vol. II, 1867.

98 Francis Buchanan-Hamilton, A journey from Madras through Mysore, Canara and Malabar, Vol. 2, 1807.

metal objects. These included a copper plate charter issued to the temple by the Chola king Rajendra in 1036, several bells, some ritual tripods and twenty-three bronzes of a variety of Shaiva deities, all of which had been carefully laid face down within a brick pit and covered with sand. The fact that they were not recovered soon after their burial would suggest that no one involved had lived to reveal the secret of their whereabouts. [Pp. 236-237][99]

From these records, it is apparent that Muslim raids into Pandya country after Malik Kafur need to be looked at to evaluate the story of Malik Kafur and Madurai.

Later raids:

Madurai did not escape the attention of Delhi sultanate after Malik Kafur's retreat. When Muhammad bin Tughlaq successfully defeated the Kakatiya ruler Prataparudra in 1323, he turned his attention on Hoysala of Dwarasamudra and the Pandya kingdom. By 1327, he was successful in bringing these southern provinces under his influence. After his conquests, these provinces were divided into five domains viz., Devagiri (earlier Yadava), Tiling (earlier Kakatiya), Kampili, Dwarasamudra (earlier Hoysala) and Ma'bar (north Kerala, Tondaimandalam and Madurai)[100] and governors were appointed by him. With the rise of Vijayanagara in 1336, these domains ruled by Muslim governors showed varying degrees of loyalty so much so that Jalaudin Hasan Shah, governor of Ma'bar started minting his own coins and renounced sovereignty of Tughlaq by 1333-34[101]. Madurai Sultanate created by Jalaudin Hasan Shah lasted till 1378. The last ruler was Sikander Khan.

Many a travellers to South India during that time note that the rule of Madurai Sultanate was anything but just and sultans took special pleasure in destroying and vandalizing Hindus and temples in their territory. Ibn Battuta[102] and Gangadevi (wife of Kumara Kampana of Sri Rangam fame) both record the extensive violence caused by Madurai Sultanate on Hindu folk.

---

99 Allen, Charles (2017). Coromandal: A Personal History, London: Little, Brown p 236
100 Ibid, p 213.
101 Ibid, p 215.
102 Dunn, Ross E. (2005), The Adventures of Ibn Battuta, University of California Press, ISBN 978-0-520-24385-9

Kumara Kampana, son of Bukka I, finally conquered Madurai and annexed it to the Vijayanagara Empire. He also appointed a Nayak (ruler) on behalf of the Empire. Initially as vassals of the empire, Madurai Nayak became rulers of Madurai on their own accord sometime in 1529 and lasted till 1736.

However, the story of Goddess Meenakshi whose garbhagriha was stone walled by sivachariars remained a mystery during all these decades. No one survived to report Muhammad bin Tughlaq's invasion and therefore it was presumed that the Goddesses' image damaged by Malik Kafur's forces was indeed the original.

As for the original idol, there is a local lore that says the presence of original garbhagriha behind a wall was brought to the knowledge of priests of Meenakshi Temple only after victorious installation of Vijayanagara Nayak at Madurai. An old but blind man who lived near Madurai visited the temple and informed the priests that original garbhagriha was stone walled during the raid of the Muslim invaders. With the permission of Nayak ruler, it was decided to take down the rear wall of existing garbhagriha. To the delight of the Nayak and city of Madurai, original garbhagriha was revealed with Madurai Meenakshi's idol in its pristine glory.

The Nayak rulers caused prahara and temple to be renovated and sanctified, a fact that is attested by historical records.

As for the elderly blind man who revealed the secret about garbhagriha (sanctum), no evidence is as yet available, though actual occurrences appear to support the same.

7
Tipu, Marathas and Sringeri Matha

In June 1790, English East India Company forces and Maratha forces commenced the Third Anglo-Mysore War against Tipu Sultan. Captain Little's Bombay Army and Maratha armies led by Parasurambhau proceeded from Tasgaon, Maharashtra. They first attacked Dharwar in September. Dharwar held till December and then fell to invading forces. Maratha forces also composed of *Pindaris* who were notorious for looting and destruction of whole towns and villages. While it is claimed that Pindaris acted on their own, it is apparent that their operations had either explicit or implicit consent. After Dharwar, they proceeded down south and eventually arrived at Sringeri.

Pic above: Sri Vidyaranya Mahaswami being accorded royal honour in the Adda-Pallaki by the Vijayanagara Emperors, Harihara and Bukkaraya. A 17th century painting based on the mural at Virupaksha temple at Hampi. This tradition has continued since then and is followed even today. Source: https://sringeri.net/history

Swami Sachithananda Bharathi who was the head of the Mutt there, was a descendent of an illustrious line of pontiffs whose origins date back to Sri

Sureshwaracharya[103], the first disciple of Adi Shankara himself. The Mutt was itself established by Adi Shankara (788-820) and is considered first among the four main Mutts established by him at Kedarnath, Dwarka, Puri and Sringeri. Sringeri became a centre for great scholarship and prominence under its 12th pontiff, Swami Vidyaranya, who was also Acharya (guru or spiritual guide) to Harihara I who founded Vijayanagara Empire.

Sringeri Acharyas are also the Raja guru (the adviser to the king) of Mysore Wadiyar dynasty, even today.

In June 1791, Pindaris operating with Parsurambhau reached Sringeri. Under royal patronage of Vijayanagara and kings of Mysore earlier, the Mutt was richly endowed with Sri Sharadhamba temple, and other valuables of various descriptions including an elephant. Pindaris systematically set about looting and desecrating the temple and Mutt. Pleadings of the residents and Sri Sachithananda Bharathi swami fell on deaf ears. Every valuable item including idol of the goddess, jewels, gold and silver as well as the elephant were taken away. A much perturbed Sri Sachithananda Bharathi swami declared that he will fast unto death on the banks of Tungabhadra River that flows by the side of the desecrated temple. News of the vandalization of temple and Mutt reached the ears of Tipu Sultan at Mysore.

In July 1791, Tipu Sultan wrote to Sri Sachithananda Bharathi Swami of Sringeri that he was deeply dismayed over the loot and destruction caused by Maratha forces[104]. He pledged to retrieve all the loot from marauders and restore them.

Following is recorded in the Sri Sharada Peeta Sringeri website[105]:

> *Tipu, who succeeded Hyder, was opposed by the Marathas, the Nizam and the British. In the course of the campaigns of the Third Mysore War (1790 - 1792), Parasuram Bhau marched on Bednur. His hosts commanded by a Patwardan foolishly plundered Sringeri. In the letter commiserating the Acharya, Tipu wrote, "People who sin against such a holy place will at no*

---

103 Sri Sureshwaracharya is the name given to Mandana Mishra whom Adi Shankara won over through a debate that lasted for eight days at Mahishmatipura in the Maghada Empire. For the full story about this debate, see: https://sringeri.net/jagadgurus/sri-sureshwaracharya

104 Shastry, AK (2009). The Records of the Sringeri Dharmasamsthana, Sringeri: Sringeri Matha, p 171.

105 https://sringeri.net/jagadgurus/sri-sacchidananda-bharati-iii-1770-1814. Also see: https://www.deccanchronicle.com/151113/nation-current-affairs/article/tipu-sultan-protected-sringeri-math-kalkuni-vittal-hegde

distant date suffer the consequences of their misdeeds. Treachery to the Gurus will lead to all round ruin of the family." He aided in the restoration of the temple and the re-consecration of the image of Sri Sharada.

On several occasions Tipu sought the blessings of the Acharya. He once wrote that he depended upon three sources of the strength – God's grace, the Jagadguru's blessings and the strength of his arms. He requested the Acharya to perform Satachandi and Sahasrachandi japa and homa. In the subsequent letter the Sultan acknowledged the miraculous effects of the Yaga that led to success in his enterprise and how rains poured and the land flourished.

The Acharya decided to go to Poona to seek redress for the spoliation of the Mutt. Tipu invited him to Srirangapatnam before proceeding to Poona. Not having heard from the Acharya for a long time after he reached Poona, Tipu requested in a letter expressing his conviction that wherever a godly personage like Acharya stayed, there was sure to be prosperity. After returning to Sringeri, the Acharya set out on a pilgrimage to Tirupati, and other holy places. While the Acharya was at Kanchi, Tipu requested him to bless his charities to the temples there and work of renovating the temples partly destroyed during his father's campaigns.

Tipu even desired to make a pilgrimage to Sringeri, but the desire was not fulfilled. Between 1791 and 1798 Tipu wrote twenty-nine letters to the Acharya, and every one of them breathed the high veneration he had for the latter.

It is remarkable that Tipu's enemies also sought the blessings of the Acharya. Nizam-Ul-Mulk, the founder of the Asaf Jahi dynasty in Hyderabad, evinced very high respect for the Sringeri Guru and issued several special privileges on the Mutt. In 1800 Peshwa Baji Rao II communicated his decision that agrapuja should be paid to the Sringeri Sharada Peetham in all religious assemblies. He further declared himself a disciple of the Mutt. During 1785-86, Basavappa Nayak of Jugali (Anekal taluk), Basavappa Nayak of Santebennur and Chamaraja Wodeyar of Mysore conveyed their respects to the Acharya with presents and grants.

Tipu's forces pursued Pindaris and troops of Parsurambhau. Routing them in battle, they successfully retrieved most of the items taken from Sringeri. The marauders however had melted the idol and many of the jewels. Restoring them to Sringeri, Tipu commissioned a new golden idol[106] to be made for the temple and made rich grants so that the Mutt could revert to its former glory.

> To,
>
> The Honorable Shringeri Shri Sacchidananda Swamigal, bestowed with Shrimat Param Hansa.
>
> We received your letter and have understood the gravity of the matter. We have noted that the cavalry of the Maratha king attacked Sringeri and beat the Brahmins and the other people, removed the idol of the Goddess Sharda Ammanavaru (Mother) and also looted the valuables belonging to the Shringeri Math. We have also noted that four discip;les belonging to the Shringeri Math had to take shelter at Karkala and that the idol of Shringeri Sharda Ammanavaru was consecrated in ancient times and if this idol has to be consecrated again, the support of the government is needed. The reconsecration of the deity will be performed along with mass feeding, if the requisite amount is provided by the Government.
>
> Those who have committed such atrocities will suffer the consequences as stated in a particular shloka (verse in Samskrita) – 'People do evil smiling but will suffer the penalty in torments of agony – Hasadhvi Kriyathe Karma Raudhrir Anubhuyathe'. Treachery to Gurus will lead to all round ruin, destruction of all wealth and the ruin of the family.
>
> On hearing of the attack, the Sarkar has sent an elephant with it's Mahavat, Ahammed. The Asaf of the city has been ordered to get a palanquin made for the Math and pay 200 rahathis in cash and 200 rahathis for paddy for the consecration of the idol of Sri Sharada Ammanavauru. Carry out appropraite measures for the consecration of the idol of the Ammanavaru idol and send the report immediately. May God bless the government of Tipu (Ahmadi).
>
> We are sending a heavy sari (worked in Gold) and a blouse piece for the Goddess Sharada Ammanavaru, and a pair of shawls for you. Please write on receiving them. An order is sent to the Asaf of the town to deal with the problems of the Math. Contact him.
>
> Date 26, month Samarisala Babarabadhi, Year San 1219, Mahammad, Virodhikrita Samvat Ashadha Bahula 12. Writer Narasaiah. Signed Nabi Malikm

Source: https://www.reddit.com/r/bengaluru_speaks/comments/qqv172/letter_written_by_tippu_sultan_to_sringeri/

The Peshwa at Pune was equally upset over actions of Pindaris and lack of control by Parshurambhau. He even requested Sri Sachithananda Bharathi to

---

106 Shastry, AK (2009). The Records of the Sringeri Dharmasamsthana, Sringeri: Sringeri Matha, p 177-178, 181.

visit Pune so as to offer his apologies and provide appropriate relief[107]. When the guru decided to go to Pune, Tipu advised the Swami to seek 6000000 rupees[108] as compensation. Records reveal that the Peshwa indeed receive the Swami with much respect and caused Parashurambhau to restore 4800000 rupees to the Mutt.

Events concerning these are recorded in letters written by Tipu and the Swami. These letters in Kannada with English translation could be found in a book published by Sringeri Matha, authored by AK Shastry[109]

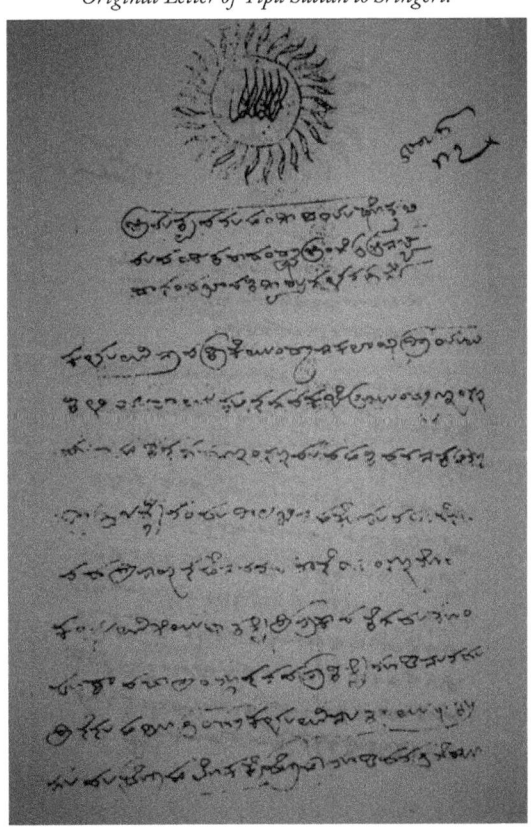

Original Letter of Tipu Sultan to Sringeri.

Source: https://www.reddit.com/r/bengaluru_speaks/comments/qqv172/letter_written_by_tippu_sultan_to_sringeri/

---

107   Ibid, p 172.
108   Ibid, p 190.
109   Shastry, AK (2009). The Records of the Sringeri Dharmasamsthana, Sringeri: Sringeri Matha

8
Vidyaranya and the Making of Vijayanagara Empire

Harihara I and Bukka I were born to Bhavana Sangama and Maravve Nayakiti, daughter of the ruler of Kampili, a vassal state under Kakatiya of Warangal. Sangama was chieftain of a cowherd community that claimed its descent from Yadava clan to which Lord Krishna is said to belong to[110]. Sangama also had three more sons by the name Kampa I, Marappa and Muddappa[111].

Harihara and Bukka entered into service of the Kakatiya kings and during Malik Kafur's southern raids in 1311, they were part of the efforts of Prataparudra, king of Kakatiya in challenging the invasion.

Kampili faced the brunt of Muslim invasion again when Muhammad bin Tughlaq, Prince Ulugh Khan at that time, first defeated Yadava of Devagiri (Daulatabad) and then Kakatiya of Warangal in 1323. Prataparudra surrendered and was despatched to Delhi. He is said to have committed suicide while at the banks of Narmada River, not willing to appear before Delhi sultan. After Warangal, Tughlaq turned his attention on Hoysala kingdom in Dwarasamudra. Kampili was situated on the way to Dwarasamudra.

After fall of Prataparudra, Harihara and Bukka took up service under raja of Kampili. When Kampili fell in 1327/28[112] [113] to Muhammad bin Tughlaq,

---

110 Sen, Sailendra (2013). A Textbook of Medieval Indian History. Primus Books. pp. 103–106. ISBN 978-9-38060-734-4.

111 Sewell, Robert (2011). A Forgotten Empire (Vijayanagar). New Delhi: Asian Educational Services. ISBN 978-8120601253. Pp 22-23.

112 It is recorded that the men of Kampili fell in battle after the women committed jauhar to save their honour and escape capture Muslim forces. See: Storm, Mary (2015). Head and Heart: Valour and Self-Sacrifice in the Art of India, New Delhi: Routledge, p 239.

113 Sastri, KAN (1975). A History of South India: From Prehistoric Times to the fall of Vijayanagara, New Delhi: Oxford University Press, p 215.

Harihara and Bukka were taken prisoner and despatched to Delhi. In the meanwhile, Prince Ulugh Khan continued his campaign in Hoysala country, proceeded into Pandya country at Madurai and looted Sri Rangam. When he returned to Delhi, the mammoth loot was much appreciated by the father, Ghiasuddin Tughlaq, sultan of Delhi.

At Delhi, Harihara and Bukka were forcibly converted to Islam. But their ability and service at Kampili was duly noted by the sultan. Adopting a strategy of appointing appeased Hindu kings as vassals in his empire, the sultan decided to send Harihara and Bukka to Kampili where they can hold the frontier for the Delhi Sultanate[114]. Thus, sometime in 1331-32, Harihara and Bukka returned to Kampili, this time as vassals of Delhi.

Once they arrived at Kampili, they began to realize implications of religious persecution and vandalization of Hindu temples by the sultanate. Apparently moved by their resolve to protect Hindu belief, they went to Anegundi to found a state of their own. Anegundi became the seed for Vijayanagara Empire as a bulwark against the Muslim rulers of North India. It ruled over South India from 1336 to 1646.

Tradition and lore present many versions of Vidyaranya's influence on Harihara and Bukka towards establishing the empire at Anegundi.

Version 1:

Swami Vidyaranya who was born as Madhava at Warangal in 1280 or 1285 had taken sanyas and was in deep meditation in the jungles around Anegundi. Once during his walk through the forest, Vidyaranya was astounded to see a hare retorting back on a hound that was trying to hunt and courageously chasing it away. He pondered about this land where a hare could valiantly chase a hound. Harihara who was hunting in the forest met Swami Vidyaranya at that time. Harihara recognized the great saint and expressed his desire to protect Hindu faith.

Swami Vidyaranya pointed to the incident of hare and the hound, and asked Harihara to found a state in the very place where the soil empowered even a humble hare to beat a hound. Harihara and Bukka then settled at the very place and developed it into Vijayanagara, the capital of the future empire.

---

114 Subrahmanyam, S. (1998). Reflections on State-Making and History-Making in South India, 1500-1800. Journal of the Economic and Social History of the Orient, 41(3), 382–416. http://www.jstor.org/stable/3632419

Version 2:

Harihara and Bukka were already disciples of Swami Vidyaranya. While at Kampili as its ruler, Harihara had gone hunting in the forests adjoining Anegundi. After a while, Harihara rested under a tree near the Virupaksha temple. His hound located a hare and started chasing it. To Harihara's utter disbelief, this hare instead of being scared of the hound attacked it ferociously, making the hound turn around and retreat. When Harihara narrated this to Swami Vidyaranya, he immediately recognized that this would be the place where Vijayanagara should be founded[115]. He guided Harihara and Bukka accordingly, predicting that the empire would last for 400 years.

Version 3:

This version follows from an exclusive monograph by Lennart Bes of Leiden University, Holland, who had relied upon sources mentioned in the footnote[116] below. The sources are as listed in page 55 of the Monograph by Lennart Bes.

---

115 Hospet Online (October 14, 2020). Myth or History of Vijayanagara? The Rivetting Story of a Hare chasing a Hound, See: https://hospet.online/history-of-vijayanagara/

116 Jackson, Vijayanagara Voices, 2-9, 14 (ns 12, 19); Nilakanta Sastri and Venkataramanayya, Further Sources of Vijayanagara History, vol. III, 6-15; Sewell, A Forgotten Empire, 16-23, 291-300; Rubiés, Travel and Ethnology in the Renaissance, 259-63; Heras, Beginnings of Vijayanagara History; Venkata Ramanayya, Vijayanagara; Srikantaya, Founders of Vijayanagara; Kulke, "Mahārājas, Mahants and Historians"; Wagoner, Tidings of the King, 33-50, 77-86, 165-9, 181-90; idem, "Harihara, Bukka, and the Sultan"; Nobuhiro ota, "Who Built 'the City of Victory'? Representation of a 'Hindu' Capital in an 'Islamicate' World," in Crispin Bates and Minoru Mio (eds), Cities in South Asia (London/New York, 2015); Subrahmanyam, Penumbral Visions, 187-92; M.H. Rāma Sharma, The History of the Vijayanagar Empire: Beginnings and Expansion (1308-1569), ed. M.H. Gopal, vol. I (Bombay, 1978), 10-23; Nilakanta Sastri, A History of South India, 233-41; Anna Libera Dallapiccola (ed.) and C.T.M. Kotraiah (trans.), King, Court and Capital: An Anthology of Kannada Literary Sources from the Vijayanagara Period (New Delhi, 2003), 24; Verghese, "Deities, Cults and Kings at Vijayanagara," 41921; Sohoni, "The Hunt for a Location," 226-7; Eaton, A Social History of the Deccan, chs 1-2; Mahalingam, Mackenzie Manuscripts, vol. II, 43-4; Dinnell, "Sāmrājyalakṣmīpīṭhikā," 57. See also B.A. Dodamani, Gaṅgādevī's Madhurāvijayaṁ: A Literary Study (Delhi, 2008), 3-7, for an interesting version of which the source is unfortunately not mentioned. see: BL/AAS, MG, no. 3, pt. 1: "Sketch of the general history of the peninsula," ff. 45-6 (probably translated from a Telugu text collected in 1801 from the Brahmins "Auhobala Sastry" and "Yanam Acharee" at the town of "Paughur," perhaps Pavagada west of Penukonda; see ff. 19, 23 and Cotton, Charpentier, and Johnston, Catalogue of Manuscripts in European Languages, vol. I, pt. II, 29); no. 11, pt. 3b: "History of the kings of Beejanagur & Anagoondy," ff. 13-16 (see also Mackenzie, "History of the Kings of Veejanagur"); no. 40, last pt.: "History of the kings of Beejayanagurr," ff. 357-70 (translated from a Telugu text in 1797, in turn translated by Brahmins at Nellore from a Sanskrit version palm-leaf text, see ff. 353-5 and Cotton, Charpentier, and Johnston, Catalogue of Manuscripts in European Languages, vol. I, pt. II, 400); MT, class VII, no. 23: "Chronological account of Bijayanagar," ff. 130-3.

One of the myth's versions has it that one day, while sleeping in a forest, Harihara had a dream in which a wise man presented him with a liṅgam, Shiva's phallic symbol, saying it would bring him prosperity, victory, and a kingdom. On another occasion, when the brothers were hunting in the forests on the river's southern bank, close to a shrine of Virupaksha, a hare turned against the dogs that were chasing it and bit them. The great Brahmin sage Vidyaranya, meditating nearby, explained that this event demonstrated the great power of this spot, where no enemy could harm even the weak. A city and a kingdom should therefore be founded here[117].

In one tradition, this foundation had already been foretold to Vidyaranya by several deities and seers during a pilgrimage to Benares on the Ganga River (Varanasi on the Ganges). In yet an earlier stage, the sage tried to gain a vision of the Goddess Bhuvaneshvari in order to attain wealth, but his efforts proved unsuccessful. Disappointed, Vidyaranya renounced the world and became a hermit. Only then did Goddess Bhuvaneshvari finally appear to him and grant his wish to be showered with gold from the sky to make the future kingdom prosper. According to some texts, now that the hour to found the city had come, Vidyaranya determined the precise rituals and perfect time for the occasion. Exactly at the most auspicious moment, the sage would blow a conch shell from some distance upon which the founding ceremony was to commence. But a nearby wandering monk, announcing his begging for alms, happened to blow his own conch shell just a bit earlier. Vidyaranya's confused assistants now executed the prescribed rituals too soon, in consequence of which the city would not exist for 3,600 glorious years, but instead survive for only 360 less glorious years. Nevertheless, the city's first king, Harihara, started constructing palaces, temples, and fortifications, moved his people there, and named the place "Vidyanagara" after the sage. After a reign of many years, he was succeeded by his brother Bukka[118].

Swami Vidyaranya served as the minster for Harihara for nearly seven years and guided him to consolidate his dominions. He moved to Sringeri Mutt eventually in 1374 where he served as the pontiff for 12 years till 1386[119].

---

117   Bes, Lennart (2022). The Heirs of Vijayanagara: Court Politics in Early Modern South India, Leiden: Leiden University Press, Pp. 54.

118   Ibid. p 55.

119   Gooding, Robert A. (2013), "A Theologian in a South Indian Kingdom: The Historical Context of the Jivanmuktiviveka of Vidyaranya", in Lindquist, Steven E. (ed.), Religion and Identity in South Asia and Beyond: Essays in Honor of Patrick Olivelle, Anthem Press.

The Sringeri Mutt website contains a full account of his life and acclaims him as the source of strengthening the Mutt, its administration and for his exceptional theological works[120]. Some of his important works are: Veda Bhashya (Commentary on the four Vedas), Sarvadarshanam, Anubhuti Prakashanam, Brahma Gita, Panchadashi, Jivan-mukti-viveka, Drik-drishya-viveka, An elaborate commentary on Parashara Smriti, Jaimaneya Nyaya-Mala-Vistara (a thesis on the Logic of Ritualism), Achara Madhavam, Vyavahara Madhavam, Shri Sankara Digvijayam, Sankara Vilasam, Upanishad Dipika[121].

Each version of the story of Swami Vidyaranya and the founding of Vijayanagara presents some facts: That Swami Vidyaranya was indeed the spiritual guide and mentor to Harihara and Bukka, that Harihara and Bukka went on to establish one of the greatest empires known in Indian history, and that the empire lasted nearly 400 years (as predicted).

This again serves as an example for the confluence of oral traditions with evidence based history, both inseparable in Indian context.

---

120 https://sringeri.net/jagadgurus/sri-vidyaranya/biography

121 Prasad, Tapovan (June 22, 2020). The Story of Vidyaranya, Chinmaya International Foundation, Blog at https://blog.chinfo.org/story-of-vidyaranya/

9
The Story of Alipiri (Tirumala)

Mir Jumla II (1591 – 30 March 1663) was born to a poor oil merchant family in Isfahan, Persia, in 1591. Through a life spanning 72 years, he rose to be an important bulwark of Aurangzeb's empire. As the emperor's governor in Bengal, he conquered the North East, spread Islam in the east and eventually died near Mankachar in Assam on 30 march 1663. He is said to have been exceptionally tall and even his grave is unusually long, as seen near Mankachar.

Mir Jumla initially arrived in Golconda kingdom as an employee of a diamond merchant with extensive dealings with sultanate. Through his capacity he rose quickly and indulged in extensive diamond trade himself. He became rich and even employed his own ships to trade with foreign shores. In due course he entered the service of Abdullah Qutb Shah of Golconda and was his all-powerful prime minister.

In 1644, Golconda felt that the Dutch at Pulicat who had been given licence to trade, were not being truthful in remitting their taxes. Mir Jumla despatched a chieftain by name 'Casey Ali' to bring Pulicat under control. However, the Dutch were able to repel the forces, apparently with some help from Nayak ruler of Vellore who claimed suzerainty over those domains. Mir Jumla then embarked upon an expedition in 1646 to bring the Nayak under Golconda rule. It was also realized that the Nayak was supported by Nayaks of Tanjore and Madurai. Hence, the help of sultan Adil Shah of Bijapur was sought. At this time, both Adil Shah and Qutb Shah were nominally feigning allegiance to Emperor Shah Jahan at Delhi and therefore, their alliance was approved by Delhi.

The Adil Shahi and Qutb Shahi forces set out to conquer entire Karnatak (the east coast region comprising of the dominions of the Nayaks of Vellore, Senji, Tanjore and Madurai). They agreed to share the booty obtained during the expedition as 2/3rd and 1/3rd respectively. Mir Jumla ran over the entire east coast between June and December 1646. His forces had also captured vast territories to the south of Nellore, area around Fort St. George at Madras, Chandragiri and Tirupati. Watching these events closely, the Dutch at Pulicat sued for peace by submission of taxes on 11 December 1646.

It is during that time that a chieftain by name Ali (presumably the same 'Casey' Ali or Ghazi Ali) attempted to reach Tirumala temple that had not witnessed any invasion till then. During Malik Kafur's raids in 1310-11, Tirupati had escaped unmolested. His taking of Sri Rangam and other temples at that time had also resulted in a large number of vaishnavas reaching Tirupati[122] and taking refuge in its inaccessible jungles.

When 'Casey' or Ghazi Ali arrived in 1646, priests at the temple were obviously alarmed since they were familiar with the stories of the looting of Sri Rangam and Chidambaram. The history of Pin Thodarntha Valli and Tulukka Nachiar of the time of Malik Kafur and Muhammad bin Tughlaq were already part of local lore.

They decided to use Muslim commanders' attraction of loot to their advantage and approached Ali with an offer. They pleaded that Muslim forces have to climb through mountainous areas where no paths lay to reach the temple; they also informed that being the domain of Varaha (the Lord in the avatar of a wild boar), Muslims have to pass through paths infested with wild pigs; without killing them, they may never reach the temple. Then they played a master card by offering two lakh rupees as indemnity if Muslim forces avoided all these hardships and leave the temple unmolested.

After much contemplation, Ali agreed to the offer with a condition that this amount shall be paid every year as a tribute to sultan of Golconda. The priests apparently agreed, there being no other choice. Ali returned victorious with a substantial two lakh rupees as indemnity. Mir Jumla was apparently pleased. From this time, Tirupati temple had to pay an annual fee of rupees two lakh to the ruling disposition in return to be spared the looting and desecration that was common from the time Malik Kafur had raided the temples of South India[123].

The area surrounding Tirupati remained under the control of Mir Jumla's forces and even used for expediting their forces for subsequent wars against Nayaks and for control of entire Karnatak. Tavernier, who recorded the events at Karnatak states that while he was at Tirupati on 26 August 1652, large forces

---

122 Viraraghavacharya, TKT (2003). History of Tirupati, Vol I, p. 69.
123 Ibid, p. 18.

The Story of Alipiri (Tirumala)

belonging to Mir Jumla continued to pass through the area[124].

The place from which Ali returned without attempting to plunder the temple is now known as Alipiri.

Devotee now traveling to Tirumala (temple on the hills) pass through Alipiri or commence the climbing of the hills on foot from there.

History also reveals that this system of annual tribute from Tirupati was continued by later rulers of the area including Nawab of Arcot. During the reign of Nawab Mohammed Ali Wallajah (1749-1795), owing to excessive amounts borrowed from East India Company (EIC), the Nawab vested the revenue from temples to the EIC. Thus, Tirupati temple came under direct administration by EIC from 1801 till 1845 through its Collector at Chittoor.

In 1803, Mr. Stutton who was the Collector, sent in a report that showed that the temple owned 187 villages of which 40 belonged to the various temple functionaries and 124 were under the management of Palayakkarars (Poligars).

In 1817, EIC passed Regulation VII to control and regulate the administration of temples in Madras Presidency. This Regulation was only superseded by Tirumala-Tirupati Devasthanams Act of 1932.

Quite interestingly, Colonel Bruce, Commissioner of Chittoor District in 1821, drew up a 42-clause code to regulate the affairs of Tirupati. This code came to be known as Bruce Code and was applied across EIC possessions in India, including Puri Jagannath.

Bruce Code was repealed by the Act of 1932.

---

124 Ibid, p. 26

10
Sultan Tanah Shah and Ramadasu

Bhakta Ramadasu (1620 – 1688) occupies an important place in the socio-cultural history of India, especially for his devotion to Lord Ram at Bhadrachalam in Andhra Pradesh. The temple for Sri Ram at Bhadrachalam was built by Ramadasu and is one of the most celebrated pilgrimage sites for millions of Hindus from across the subcontinent.

Ramadasu was born to Linganna Mantri and Kamamba in Nelakondapalli village in the Khammam District of Telangana. He was named Kancherla Gopanna at birth. Though his was an affluent family, Gopanna lost both his parents and led a life of penury as an orphan. As a child, he lived mostly by singing songs in praise of Sri Ram for seeking alms. He was noted for his devotion to Sri Ram. It is said that Raghunatha Bhattacharya was once passing through the village where Gopanna was seeking alms by singing the praise of Sri Ram. Hearing those melodious and surprisingly original compositions, Raghunatha Bhattacharya took him in as his disciple and trained him in the traditions of Vaishnava bhakti and inducted him into the Dasarathi traditions.

Life was not to pass as a disciple in humble surroundings for Gopanna. Two of his uncles, Madanna and Akkanna served as ministers[125] in the court of Sultan Abdullah Qutb Shah (1611-1672) of Golconda. The full names of these uncles were Madhava Bhanuji and Akkarasu Bhanuji respectively sounding much like Maratha Brahmins, though they were fluent in Telugu as well. They had assisted Abdullah Qutb Shah to ascend to the throne and enjoyed his confidence.

The Dutch records of the time note that both Madanna and Akkanna were of considerable influence at the court and the Shah depended on their advice for administration of his kingdom[126]. Qutb Shah had only three daughters and

---

125   Longhurst, A.H. (1924). Memoirs of the Archaeological Survey of India, Simla: Government of India Press, Number 17 Part 1, pp. 24

126   Kruijtzer, G. (2002). Madanna, Akkanna and the Brahmin Revolution: A Study of Mentality,

one of them was married to Abul Hasan Qutb Shah. When he died in 1672, amirs of the court helped Abul Hasan to ascend to the throne of Golconda. Abul Hasan was known as a tolerant sultan who respected other religions and practices. He was also assisted by Madanna and Akkanna in the struggle for power and therefore he retained them as ministers[127]. The retaining of Madanna and Akkanna caused serious rifts with Emperor Aurangzeb at Delhi. It was reported to Aurangzeb that this 'kafir' ministers had subjected Sayyids, Shaikhs and scholars into servitude[128], a report that would cost dearly when Aurangzeb invaded Golconda some years later. During the invasion of 1685, Aurangzeb had Madanna beheaded and Akkanna trampled under the feet of an elephant[129].

Abdullah Qutb Shah

Pic courtesy: Wiki at https://en.wikipedia.org/wiki/File:Abdullah_Qutb_Shah.jpg

But then, these events were to take place a decade or so later.

Abul Hasan Qutb Shah was also known as Tanah Shah. He was nicknamed as 'Tanah Shah' by his teacher, a Sufi saint Hazarat Shah Raju Qattal, even before he was a contender to the throne of Golconda. Abul Hassan had a good voice and sang well. He also had a certain innocence about him. Sufi Saint Shah Raju,

---

Group Behaviour and Personality in Seventeenth-Century India. Journal of the Economic and Social History of the Orient, 45(2), 231–267. http://www.jstor.org/stable/3632842

127 Aiyangar, S. Krishnaswami (1932). Abul Hasan Qutub Shah and his Ministers, Madanna and Akkanna. Journal of Indian History. University of Kerala. 10: 93–107.

128 Ibid, p 126.

129 Longhurst, A.H. (1924). Memoirs of the Archaeological Survey of India, Simla: Government of India Press, Number 17 Part 1, p. 24.

gave him the nickname of 'Tanah Shah' which means a child saint. He was also known as Tani Shah, meaning "benevolent ruler"[130].

It is said that Hazarat Qattal once playfully tossed a pomegranate at young Tanah Shah asking him as to how many seeds it had. Young Tanah, without blinking an eye answered '14'. The Hazarat smiled at him and said that he will rule for 14 years. This prophesy came true, for Tanah Shah's reign ended in 1686.

Tanah Shah

Source: https://ranasafvi.com/abul-hasan-qutb-shah-yana-shah-2/

When Tanah Shah ascended to throne of Golconda, Madanna and Akkanna took kindly to the plight of Gopanna and secured him a post of tehsildar (the revenue administrator for a sub-division responsible for land administration and revenue collection[131]). Gopanna eagerly took to his assignments and was even praised by the Sultan for his sincerity in the discharge of his duties. Apparently revenue collection soared in the tehsil of Bhadrachalam where Gopanna was in charge. He married and continued his piety to Sri Ram as well as his duty to Sultan.

During one of his official tours, he visited a fair at Bhadrachalam and saw the dilapidated condition of temple. This place holds much significance in the epic Ramayana. Ram and Sita met the aged devotee Sabari here and partook humble

---

130 Safvi, Rana (n.d.). Abul Hasan Qutb Shah/ Tana Shah,

131 This term with the same title is even now in vogue all over India. The Tehsildar's role remains the same. The term Tehsil is derived from Urdu, meaning a revenue sub-division.

fruits that she offered. Ramayana says that Sabari tasted them for their sweetness out of her love for Ram before giving to him! Ram and Sita also stayed in her ashram. Religious significance of Bhadrachalam is immense and plight of the temple therefore deeply troubled Gopanna. As he was the tehsildar, the villagers also pleaded with him to help renovate the ancient temple. At the request of the village, he agreed to provide taxes he had so far collected as a loan. He even mobilized donations to the renovation and expansion of the temple. The villagers had promised to return this loan once their harvest was over. Unfortunately, the harvest failed and Gopanna was left with the predicament of answering the sultan. In the mean while, when construction of temple was in progress, people who envied Gopanna both for his piety and the benevolence he received from Madanna and Akkanna, reported to sultan of the shortages in tax revenue. An agitated sultan ordered Gopanna to be arrested and confined him to a prison at Golconda. Gopanna was incarcerated for 12 years. During his incarceration, he composed immense paeans in praise of Lord Ram as well as poems crying his misery at incarceration that prevented him from worship of Lord Ram.

Twelve years passed and one day, two young men who claimed to have come from Ayodhya, sought to see the sultan in his court. Wondering the intention of these two young men, Tanah Shah had they produced in front of him. They claimed to be Ram and Lakshman by name and informed the Sultan that they have come to pay dues on behalf of Gopanna. They then produced gold coins in payment. The sultan was taken completely by surprise that these young men produced gold coins that amounted to entire tax revenue due to the court. Before he could ascertain further details about them, they took leave and disappeared from Golconda[132] [133].

Tanah Shah was a deeply religious person and was extremely sensitive to the belief of other religions too. He realized that Gopanna was indeed blessed to have had divine intervention. He had Gopanna released from prison and offered to reinstate him as tehsildar. Gopanna however refused, proclaiming his devotion to Lord Ram and his intention to spend remaining life at Bhadrachalam. Tanah Shah had Gopanna conveyed to Bhadrachalam on an elephant, with immense

---

[132] Glener, Doug & Komaragiri, Sarat (2002). Chapter 23: The Might of the Mighty in Wisdom's Blossoms: Tales of the Saints of India. Shambhala Publications. ISBN 978-0-8348-2938-1.

[133] Rajanikanta Rao (see note 93) states that the Dutch writers Hawart and martin noted in their books that Gopanna was released by divine intervention and Lord Rama paid the debt of six lakh varaha and even obtained a receipt from Tanah Shah with the seal of his signet ring (the royal seal). See P. 27-28 of Rao's Ramadasu cited in note 93.

presents and money for completion of the temple and for the worship of Lord Ram[134]. For his devotion to Lord Ram, Gopanna came to be known as Bhakta Ramadasu.

A different version

This version of Ramadasu slightly varies as per some local narrations/traditions and scholars. They confirm to Madanna and Akkanna being instrumental in obtaining the post of tehsildar, but under Abdullah Qutb Shah, the father-in-law and predecessor of Tanah Shah[135]. As per this tradition, Gopanna was appointed sometime in 1650 on the recommendations of Madanna and Akkanna[136] by Mir Jumla, the prime minister for Abdullah at that time. Abdullah was also so pleased by the devotion and services of Gopanna in the ensuing two years as to grant two villages, Bhadrachalam and Rekapalli, as jagirs to the temple. This was also inscribed in a stone slab maintained at Bhadrachalam temple[137].

Two years or so into his employment, Ramadasu helped construct the temple at Bhadrachalam using tax collections in his jurisdictions. When this matter was reported to the court, Tanah Shah acting in the capacity of prince, had him incarcerated[138] much against the pleadings of Madanna and Akkanna.

After the death of Abdullah Qutb Shah in 1672, Tanah Shah ascended to the throne. Madanna and Akkanna played an important role in this and were retained as ministers. They pleaded again with the new sultan and offered to deposit six lakh varaha used by Gopanna for the temple in return for the release of their nephew. Tanah Shah agreed to the proposal and had Gopanna released in 1674.

Both the versions may have variations, but they agree that Gopanna spent 12 years in prison and returned to Bhadrachalam for service to the Lord. In 1677 Tanah Shah also re-issued the firman of Abdullah Shah regarding grant of Bhadrachalam and Rekapalli as jagirs to the temple. The stone inscription regarding this was damaged by Ibrahim Khan (also known as Dhansa) in 1766,

---

134   Rao, Rajanikanta B. (1988). Ramadasu. Sahitya Akademi, Pp. 17-21

135   Glener, Doug; Komaragiri, Sarat (2002). Chapter 23: The Might of the Mighty. Wisdom's Blossoms: Tales of the Saints of India. Shambhala Publications. ISBN 978-0-8348-2938-1.

136   Rao, Rajanikanta B. (1988). Ramadasu. Sahitya Akademi, p. 19.

137   Ibid, p 20.

138   Ibid, p. 25.

when the area was under control of Nizam of Hyderabad. Ibrahim Khan futilely attempted to loot the temple at that time. Priests of the temple however managed to take the deity and valuables to Santamamilla village in Polavaram taluk where the Lord remained in exile for five years.

The Nizam was upset over the activities of Ibrahim Khan and sanctioned Rupees 40000 for restoring the temple and commencement of rituals. The Lord apparently returned to Bhadrachalam in 1761-62. Nearly seventy years later (in 1832), Thumu Narasimhadasu the raja of Guntur and Varada Ramadasu of Kanchi used their proximity with Chandulal, an advisor to Nizam Nasaraddaula, to have the stone inscription of 1677 re-issued and jagirs reinstated to Bhadrachalam[139].

Six lakh Varaha

Varaha refers to the gold coins issued by Vijayanagara Empire[140] that came to be used widely across the Deccan by all rulers well up to the end of 17th century or beginning of 18th century. Noted Muslim historian Firishta noted (in 1607 CE) that 'even up to the present day, that same infidel coinage is current among the Muslims'.[141] The varaha weighed 3.35 grams of gold[142]. By this standard, expenditure for the temple renovation undertaken by Ramadasu should have costed as below:

600000 varaha x 3.35 gm = 2010, 000 gms = 2010 kilograms of gold.

Should the income from one tehsil of Golconda be equal to 2010 kg in gold, the wealth of the sultanate may as well be imagined. It is also to be recalled that Golconda remained the only state where diamonds were harvested. Thus the combined riches of this sultanate became the reason for Aurangzeb to invade Golconda on a flimsy excuse that Mir Jumla's son was insulted by the sultan

---

139 Ibid, Pp. 28-29.

140 Desikachari, T. (1991). South Indian Coins. New Delhi: Asian Educational Services. Pp. 75-76. ISBN 978-8120601550.

141 Wagoner, P. B. (2014). Money use in the Deccan, c. 1350–1687: The role of Vijayanagara hons in the Bahmani currency system. The Indian Economic & Social History Review, 51(4), 457-480. https://doi.org/10.1177/0019464614550762

142 These coins varied slightly from 3.33 to 3.42 grams. An approximation of 3.35 has been taken. See: https://www.bombayauctions.com/searchauctionitem.aspx?auctioncode=1044&pricerange=&keyword=&category=3&material=0&lotno=

for his frivolous behaviour[143]. Mir Jumla, though he served as prime minister of Golconda, was given to vanity after his decisive victory over Devagiri (Hoysala kingdom) and the loot he managed to obtain from there. Mir Jumla's daughter was married to Aurangzeb and therefore, this incident over behaviour of Mir Jumla's son at Golconda gave him a perfect excuse to invade the sultanate, defeat and arrest Tanah Shah in 1685-86. The arrest and death of Tanah Shah brought Qutb Shahi rule in Golconda to an end forever.

Abul Qutb Shah, Tanah Shah as he is remembered, remained in prison for 12 years at Daulatabad (Devagiri) fort and died in 1699.

If Ramadasu's imprisonment of 12 years corresponds with that of Tanah Shah, it is a matter of historical coincidence.

As for the coins that Lord Ram (or Madanna and Akkanna) gave for release of Ramadasu, Bhadrachalam temple even today displays a set that depicts Ram and Sita with Hanuman, presumably at their coronation at Ayodhya:

Pic source: https://www.booksfact.com/history/bhadrachala-ramadasu-debt-tana-shah-not-paid-ramoji-lakshmoji.html

Incidentally, the Vijayanagara Empire also issued coins known as Ramatanka that depicted Lord Ram, Sita and Hanuman in the manner that the above coin depicts[144]. Considering that these coins of Vijayanagar were widely in use in the Deccan, we may presume the authenticity of the version where Madanna and Akkanna paid for the release of Ramadasu from prison. Divine intervention as noted in bhakti traditions continues to hold its merit.

---

143   Madras Courier (May 30, 2018). Tana Shah: The Last Ruler between Aurangzeb & the World, online at https://madrascourier.com/biography/tana-shah-the-last-ruler-between-aurangzeb-and-the-world/ Accessed October 24, 2023.

144   See: https://marudhararts.com/printed-auction/auction-no-25/lot-no-221/die-seal-and-tokens/tokens/hindu-taken/ram-darbar/extremely-rare-gold-scyphate-ramatanka-token-of-vijayanagara-period-.html and https://www.michaelbackmanltd.com/object/ram-darbar-temple-token-ramatanka/ for coins of similar make that have been sold in international auctions.

Madanna by unkown artist

Pic source: "Arts de l'Islam, un passé pour un présent", 20 novembre 2021 au 27 mars 2022, Rennes. Source/Photographer: photo by Pymouss (https://commons.wikimedia.org/wiki/File:Madanna_-_MBAR_20220320.jpg)

Birth Place of Bhakta Ramadasu at Nelakondapalli

Pic source: https://www.thehansindia.com/posts/index/Telangana/2016-04-15/Bhakta-Ramadasu-birthplace-forgotten/221617?infinitescroll=1

Sri Ramachandraswamy, Bhadrachalam

Pic source: https://www.divyadesam.com/photos/feb-2011/sri-ramar-bhadrachalam.shtml

Bhakta Ramadasu Idol installed by Government of Telengana on 29-1-2020 in connection with the Sri Bhakta Ramadasu Jayanthi Utsavam, in the birth place of the great vaaggeyakara, Nelakondapally, Khammam district.

Source: https://www.facebook.com/1790467801173134/posts/here-its-the-making-of-a-statue-of-sri-bhakta-ramadasu-to-be-inaugurated-tomorro/2619128088307097/

Expenditure of Six lakh Varaha

There are no records as to the expenditure of six lakh varaha for the construction of the temple. The answer to this could be discerned from an immortal sahitya that Ramadasu sang while in prison at Golconda.

Song: Ikshvaku Kula Thilaka, Raag: Yadukula kamboji, Taal: Caapu

Pallavi:
Ikshvaku kula tilaka ikanaina palukave ramachandra
Nannu rakshimpakunnanu rakshakulevarinka ramachandra

Charanam 01:
Bharatunaku jeyisti pachala patakamu ramachandra
Aa patakamunaku batte padivela varahalu ramachandra

Charanam 02:
Satrghnunakuni jeyisti molatradu ramachandra
Aa molatratiki batte mohareelu padivelu ramachandra

Charanam 03:
Lakshmanunaku jeyisti mutyala patakamu ramachandra
Aa patakamunaku batte padivela varahalu ramachandra

Charanam 04:
Seetammmaku jeyisti cimtaku patakamu ramachandra
Aa patakamunaku batte padivela varahalu ramachandra

Charanam 05:
Kalikiturayi melukuga jeyisti ramachandra
Neevu kulukucu tirigevu evarabba som&mani ramachandra

Charanam 06:
Nee tamdri dasaratha maharaju pettena ramachandra
Leka mee mama A janaka maharaju pampena ramachandra

Charanam 07:
Abba tittitinani ayasapadavaddu ramachandra
Ee debbala korvaka abba Tittinayya ramachandra

Charanam 08:
Bhaktulandarini paripalinchedi Sree ramachandra
Neevu kshemamuga Sree ramadasuni elu ramachandra

Meaning:

Pallavi:

O Ramachandra! Decoration for Ikshvaku clan! Why don't you speak at least now?

O Ramachandra! If you do not save me, who else will save me?

Charanam 01:

O Ramachandra! I made the emerald ornament for your brother Bharatha

O Ramachandra! That ornament cost ten thousand varahas

Charanam 02:

O Ramachandra! I got it made for Satrghnuna an ornament with precious stones

O Ramachandra! That ornament took ten thousand varahas to make

Charanam 03:

O Ramachandra! I got it made for Lakshmana an Pearl ornament

O Ramachandra! That ornament took ten thousand varahas to make

Charanam 04:

O Ramachandra! I got it made for Sita an ornament (that looks like a leaf of tamarind tree)

O Ramachandra! That ornament took ten thousand varahas to make

Charanam 05:

O Ramachandra! I got carefully made for you an ornament with precious stones

O Ramachandra! You are moving around enjoying it but whose money you think it is!

Charanam 06:

O Ramachandra! Did your father, King Dasaratha, gave them to you?

O Ramachandra! Or, did your father-in-law, King Janaka sent them to you?

Charanam 07:

O Ramachandra! Ha (sound when being beaten), please don't get upset at my criticism

O Ramachandra! I criticized you as I was unable to bear the pain of this beating

Charanam 08:

O Sri Ramachandra! You take care of all of your devotees

O Ramachandra! Please definitely take care of this devotee Ramadasu also

[Source: https://krishnavaibhavam.blogspot.com/2015/02/ikshvaku-kula-thilaka.html]

The song recounts that 40000 varaha was spent on jewels that Ramadasu made for Sitamma, Lakshmana, Bharata, Shatrugna. In addition, it even questions the value of jewels that adorn Sri Ram himself (for which no amount is indicated). Taken together, it can only be presumed that remaining varaha were spent for Sri Ram's jewels, construction of the temple and for instituting the rites thereabout.

11
The In-Laws of Lord Venkateshwara Swamy

Devunikadapa is a part of Kadapa town located in Kadapa district of Andhra Pradesh. Tradition says that Kripacharya, one of the teachers of Pandava and Kaurava of Mahabharata, established the temple for Sri Lakshmi Venkateshwara there. Purana mention this temple as 'Kripavathi Kshetram'[145] [146]. The temple is now under the care of Tirumala Tirupati Devasthanam (administrative body responsible for Tirupati).

Kripacharya was one of the few who survived Mahabharata war. When Pandava ascended to throne of Indraprastha, he retired to the forest to lead a life of a saint[147]. During his sojourns across this subcontinent, Kripacharya established a temple at Devuni Kadapa. In later centuries, this temple was renovated and built upon by kings of Vijayanagara. In four districts of Rayalaseema area of Andhra Pradesh, this temple is considered as holy as Tirupati Venkateshwara temple. It was also a part of Talapaka Annamacharya's songs in praise of the Lord.

Sri Lakshmi Venkateshwara Swamy temple at Devunikadapa has a unique tradition. On the occasion of Ugadi (Telugu new year day that falls on first day of Hindu lunisolar calendar month of Chaitra i.e. in the month of April), thousands of Muslims visit this temple and offer appropriate items of worship that Hindu devotees offer along with vastra (clothe) for the Lord and his consort,

---

145 Wilson, Horace Hayman (1840). The Vishnu Purana.

146 Govt of AP: YSR Panchayat (n.d.) Devuni Kadapa Sri Lakshmi Venkateswara Temple. See: https://web.archive.org/web/20150123074952/http://www.ysrkadzp.appr.gov.in/hidden/-/asset_publisher/di5XrVERUf8s/content/devuni-kadapa-sri-lakshmi-venkateswara-temple

147 Mani, Vettam (1975). Puranic encyclopaedia: a comprehensive dictionary with special reference to the epic and Puranic literature. Robarts - University of Toronto. Delhi: Motilal Banarsidass. pp. 418, 419. ISBN 9780842608220.

Lakshmi. They consider Lord Venkateshwara as their son-in-law. This tradition is in vogue for over seven centuries now.

Lord Venkateshwara, as purana state, married the daughter of Akasa Raja of Tirupati. Alamelu Manga, this spiritual consort, has a temple at Alamelu Mangapuram at Tirupati. However, Muslims of Royalaseema also believe that the Lord married Tulukka Nachiar, a princess of Mughal elite from Delhi. The versions of stories surrounding Tulukka Nachiar in Rayalaseema region are as below:

Version 1:

Bibi Nancharamma, a Muslim woman, is believed to be a wife of Lord Venkateshwara by many Muslims of Rayalaseema (a region comprising of four districts in present state of Andhra Pradesh).

After Goddess Lakshmi cursed Lord Venkateshwara and Goddess Padmavati to turn into stone, she repents her mistake. She realizes that she has insulted the Lord and decides to incarnate in a human form and win back a place in his heart with her devotion and prayer.

It is believed that she was reborn as Nancharamma to a Muslim king several centuries later. With her staunch love and worship to the Lord, she attained Moksha and adorned a place back in his heart.

Story of Lord Venkateshwara, Goddess Padmavathi and Bibi Nancharamma as believed by the priests of the temple say that Lord Balaji married a Muslim woman Bibi Nancharamma, who was the daughter of a Muslim general in 1311 AD, after he was immensely pleased by her devotion. Her idol has a pride of place in Tirumala temple precincts[148] also.

Version 2:

Muslims treat Lord Venkateshwara as their son-in-law. They believe that Lord Balaji married a Muslim woman named Bibi Nancharamma who was the daughter of a general named Malik Kafur in 1311 AD[149].

---

148   Temple Purohit (n.d.). Story of Lord Venkateswara, Padmavati and Bibi Nancharamma. See: https://www.templepurohit.com/story-venkateswara-padmavathi-bibi-nancharamma/. Accessed October 21, 2023.

149   TNM Staff (Apr 09, 2016). The Hindu temple in Andhra Pradesh where Muslims seek blessings for Ugadi. The News Minute. See: https://www.thenewsminute.com/andhra-pradesh/hindu-tem-

Version 3:

Muslims consider Bibi Nancharamma, who was married to Lord Venkateshwara, a daughter of the community. Consequently, they consider Lord Venkateshwara as their son-in-law and therefore, present gifts to their son-in-law every year on the occasion.

In an exclusive interview with Deccan Chronicle, the priests Macha Seshacharyulu and Trivikram explained that this practice has been observed over centuries and that Muslims make the first prayer every year on Ugadi day. 'Additionally, Muslim devotees present saris and other materials to their daughter Bibi Nancharamma,' they said[150].

Version 4:

Muslim devotees at Devuni Kadapa Sri Lakshmi Venkateswara Temple

A devotee Basha who came with his family members said Muslims offer prayers to the Lord and His Consort Bibi Nancharamma in a traditional manner, a practice in vogue since ages. It is a practice that is prevalent across the Rayalaseema region, and many Muslims from Chittoor, Kurnool and Anantapur district

---

ple-andhra-pradesh-where-muslims-seek-blessings-ugadi-41374. Accessed October 22, 2023.
150   Balleda, Nageshwara Rao (April 7, 2019). Muslims head for Andhra Pradesh Balaji temple, The Deccan Chrinicle. See: https://www.deccanchronicle.com/nation/current-affairs/070419/muslims-head-for-andhra-pradesh-balaji-temple.html Accessed October, 21, 2023.

also visit the temple. As Lord Venkateshwara married Bibi Nancharamma, the Muslims treat Him as their son-in-law[151].

Pic Courtesy: The News Minute https://www.thenewsminute.com/andhra-pradesh/hindu-temple-andhra-pradesh-where-muslims-seek-blessings-ugadi-41374

Note: *The history of Tulukka Nachiar narrated earlier in this book finds that she a.k.a Suradhani is related to Sri Rangam in the aftermath of Malik Kafur's raid on Sri Rangam in 1310. Considering the historical evidence presented, and the fact that Sri Ramanuja was also responsible for formalizing the ways of worship in Tirupati, we must surmise that this story of Bibi Nachiar at Tirupati as well as Rayalaseema originate from the same source. That this geographical area falls in the route of Malik Kafur and possibly the route taken by Pin Thodarntha Valli and Tulukka Nachiar add support to this premise. It is also to be noted that Malik Kafur was a eunuch and did not have even adopted children.*

---

151 Express News Service (Apr 15, 2021). Muslims pray at Kurnool temple every Ugadi, The New Indian Express. See: https://www.newindianexpress.com/states/andhra-pradesh/2021/apr/15/muslims-pray-at-kurnool-temple-every-ugadi-2290075.html Accessed October 21, 2023.

12
A Temple for Duryodhana

Kollam in Kerala is famous for cashews famed in accounts of travellers from historic times. Kollam City boasts of a long history of political, commercial and cultural importance having found mention in several ancient accounts. With a varied colonial past under Portuguese, Dutch and the British, Kollam has locations of historical importance like Thangasseri light house, St. Thomas Fort and cemetery built by Portuguese, Thevally Palace, Cheenakkottaram etc. Besides, it also has sites of several old buildings constructed by Travancore kings (its rulers during pre-Independence times) in a variety of architectural styles, where many government offices still function[152].

Kerala itself is known as Parasurama Kshetra, the land of Parasurama, an ancient rishi-warrior. As per Ramayana, this saint-warrior challenged Sri Ram at the time of Ram's marriage with Sita. These myths and legends of Kerala are therefore intrinsically woven into the fabric of Indian culture. Kerala also finds a place in Vishnupurana. Lord Vishnu is said to have taken Vamana (short or dwarfish) avatar to subdue Bali Chakravarti (Emperor Mahabali, as known in Kerala and considered as king of Kerala even now). Vamana walked in when Maha Bali was conducting a fire sacrifice (yagya). When fire sacrifices were conducted, providing things to brahmanas was considered auspicious. Mahabali therefore, offered to give Vamana what he desired. Vamana in turn, merely asked for three foot of land. Mahabali immediately took a vessel containing water and proceeded to pour the water into Vamana's hands as a sign of confirming the grant. Shukracharya, guru of Mahabali, realised that this was a trick by Lord Vishnu to banish Mahabali to patala loka (the nether land). He attempted to block nozzle of the vessel from which Mahabali was pouring water into Vamana's hand. Vamana then took a small grass and inserted into the nozzle, blinding and forcing Shukracharya to give up his attempt.

---

152   Govt. of Keral (n.d.). Kollam District. See: https://kollam.nic.in/en/about-district/#:~:text=Kollam%20has%20been%20the%20centre,processed%20cashew%20exporter%20in%20India. Accessed October 23, 2023.

Having secured the grant, Vamana then grew into a colossal form that took all the worlds in merely two steps. When asked as to where should he place his third step, Mahabali realized that Vamana was none other than Lord Vishnu himself. He joyously offered his own head for the third step and Vamana pressed Mahabali into the nether world. Lord Vishnu however was pleased by the sincerity of Mahabali and granted a boon – Mahabali can return to his country (Kerala) once a year and be the king for a day.

Wamana Avatar, a Dutch Painting dating to 1672, Wellcome Library, London.

Source: https://en.wikipedia.org/wiki/File:Vamana_teaching_King_Mahabali_Wellcome_V0050544.jpg

Onam festival that is celebrated in Kerala marks the day Mahabali returns to Kerala every year. It falls on the first day of the month of Chingam in Malayalam Calendar (Aug-September)[153]. Malayali diaspora including, Onam is an important festival of Kerala marking many days of celebrations. It is a time when entire state is decked up with Athapookkalam and lights. Visitors to Kerala during this festive season have an opportunity to experience the hospitality

---

153 Cush, Denise; Robinson, Catherine; York, Michael (2012). Encyclopedia of Hinduism. Routledge. pp. 573–574. ISBN 978-1-135-18979-2.

and culture of the state on a first-hand basis. With boat races, Onasadhya, Athachamayam, Pulikali, Kummattikali, Thumbi Thullal and Onam Sadya, this festival also showcases artistic and cultural diversity[154] of Kerala.

Amidst these myths and legends concerning Kerala, there is one that provokes immense wonder – the story of Duryodhana of Mahabharatha. This grand epic records that five sons of Pandu (Pandava) were banished to the forest for fourteen years by Duryodhana when the eldest of Pandava, Yudhistra, lost a game of dice to Duryodhana. One of the conditions attending to this banishment was the last year of the banishment will be *agnyatavasa* (residence in secret or unkown to others). Should these five brothers be discovered during this last year, they will forfeit the claim to throne forever.

Thirteen years of the banishment passed with much events and Pandava brothers even managed to save Duryodhana himself when he was abducted by Gandharva. However, the last year of agnyatavasa was a real challenge and the brothers took immense care to live in disguise.

Having lost his many plots to get them killed in the forests earlier, Duryodhana determines to find them during the last year. It will be a permanent end to their claims for the throne. He set out with a great army and scoured the subcontinent intensely. While at the southern tip of the continent in due course, he got separated from his forces.

Roaming in deep jungles and desolate areas, he eventually reached Malanad (near Kollam). Tired and hungry, he collapsed to the ground and concluded that his end indeed was near. Thirst parched his throat and he was lying motionless when a Kurava woman of the area passed by with a pitcher on her head. Duryodhana called out to her to give something to drink and save him from parching thirst.

The woman recognized him as a royal by his clothes, who by the customs of the country was prime among the castes. She being an untouchable, would face certain death if she provided anything to him to drink or eat. But seeing his condition, she resolved to save his life even if it meant giving up hers. She offered the pitcher containing toddy, fresh from coconut trees.

Duryodhana drank heartily and soon was fully recovered. Immensely pleased, he addressed the woman as 'amma' (mother), thanking her for saving

---

154 Govt. of Kerala, Department of Tourism (n.d.). Onam: The Legend of Mahabali. See: https://www.keralatourism.org/onam/history/mahabali-legend. Accessed October 23, 2023.

his life. The Kurava woman submitted her life to him, stating that she had done her duty and now he must do his by cleaving her head, for she had committed the crime of breaching caste codes.

Duryodhana was moved by her sincerity and proclaimed that he would not only let her live, but protect her whole clan forever. So saying, he sat on a rock nearby and prayed to Lord Shiva to grant him his wish of protecting the clan of that woman.

The clan of Kurava built a temple in honour of Duryodhana at the spot where he meditated. The temple stands even today. During an annual festival[155] to commemorate Duryodhan, thousands congregate and pray in the temple. The land on which the temple is built is registered in the name of 'Duryodhan' and even now land tax is paid in his name. The temple is known as Poruvazhy Peruviruthy Malanada Temple, which about 29 km north east of Kollam[156].

The Temple of Duryodhana, Poruvazhy

The cultural mosaic of India is indeed a wonder for it is so inclusive as to defy ordinary understanding of religion, customs and belief in the sense that the world otherwise perceives.

---

155 Poruvazhy Peruviruthy Malanada Temple (n.d.). Malakkuda. See: https://malanada.com/festivals/malakkuda

156 TOI (Feb 15, 2021). A look at India's only Duryodhana Temple in Kerala, Times of India. See: https://timesofindia.indiatimes.com/travel/things-to-do/a-look-at-indias-only-duryodhana-temple-in-kerala/articleshow/80822807.cms Accessed Oct 23, 2023.

A Temple for Duryodhana

The Festival for Duryodhana. Pic Courtesy: www.malanada.com/gallery

The temple for Duryodhana, considered as villain extraordinary in Indian epics lives on as the saviour of thousands who continue to believe that he is their protecting deity.

13
Robert Clive's Makarakandi

In many ways the second Carnatic War of 1751 defined and determined the course of history in the subcontinent. It conferred an aura of invincibility on British arms that few princes in India dared challenge in subsequent times. It laid the first building blocks of an empire 'where the Sun never set'. It gave Great Britain an unassailable control over affairs of the world, major parts of which it ruled for the next two hundred years. And, there was one single 'clerk' of East India Company who laid this foundation for an empire - Robert Clive.

Clive has been much praised and equally maligned for the grit, courage and enviable enterprise that he displayed in the service of this Empire. His exploits in Carnatic and later in Plassey (West Bengal) paved the way for his meteoric rise. He retired to England as Major General Lord Robert Clive, KB, and FRS along with the name "Clive of India" and millions of pounds in his personal treasury.

In August 1751, little did he know a future that awaited him when he approached Thomas Saunders, Governor of Madras, with a proposal to attack Arcot, the capital of Nawab of Arcot. A contender to Arcot throne, Chanda Sahib, was assisted by French from Pondicherry. With Asif Jha Nizam of Hyderabad dead and a war of succession in Nizam's domains including Arcot raging, the French had usurped their rivalry with British by strongly backing Chanda Sahib. A hesitant support from British to Muhammed Ali Walajah, rightful successor to the throne at Arcot was hardly sufficient for Walajah to hold out at his fort at Trichy. Having secured Arcot for himself with French help, Chanda Sahib had laid a siege to Trichy and all odds were against Walajah. The English Directors at Calcutta had actually conceded to the supremacy of French, resigning themselves to the loss of their influence in southern parts. Thomas Saunders had very little forces to supplement Walajah or to out manoeuvre Chanda Sahib.

In this gloomy scenario, Clive approached Saunders with an imaginatively bold plan: attack Arcot to relieve pressure on Walajah. After considerable deliberations, Saunders relieved 200 of 350 British soldiers and a further 300 Indian sepoys from Fort St George. He could place only three cannons at the disposal of Clive. An unfazed Clive set course to Arcot with the tiniest army that he could thus muster. Arcot lay 69 miles South-South West from Madras. Commencing his forced march on 26 August 1751, Clive reached Conjeevaram (Kanchipuram) a distance of 42 miles on 29 August. And, the earth shook not from the pounding heels of marching columns or from a mile long train of support elements, but from a thunder storm that lashed Conjeevaram. Camping near Varadaraja temple, overseeing the securing of his troops and munitions, an exhausted Clive fell to the earth shivering. His body burned and his followers realized that he was seized by fevers common in India. English medical help in his troop could hardly relieve him of his suffering. As the night wore, troops feared the worst for him.

Some of his Indian sepoys approached a bhattar (priest) of Varadaraja temple. After seeing Clive's condition, this priest administered a dose of 'Thulasi theertha' (holy water with basil leaves used in the worship of Vishnu). He assured Clive that Varadaraja, the Lord of Conjeevaram, would cure and protect him. By sunrise, Clive felt rejuvenated and full of life. He decided to offer obeisance to Varadaraja and entered the temple after cleansing himself. He thanked Varadaraja and prayed for victory at Arcot. He also wowed to present to Varadaraja the most valuable thing that he comes across in Arcot treasury after he wins the fort.

Refreshed and alive, Clive force marched again to Arcot through a thunderstorm, covering remaining 27 miles in two days. Chanda Sahib's garrison at Arcot panicked at the approach of English troops and fled. They left behind a huge cache of arms, canons and the treasury.

Sir John Malcolm who wrote a three volume book on the life of Robert Clive, basing his narration from personal papers and diaries in the possession of Lord Clive's family, describes these events in following words:

> *Fort St. David and Madras were left, the one with 100, the other with less than 50 men, in order to supply the greatest force that could be collected for this enterprise. The detachment, when completed, nevertheless, consisted of no more than 300 sepoys and 200 Europeans, with eight officers, six of whom*

> *had never before been in action; and four of these six were young men in the mercantile service of the Company, who, inflamed by his example, took up the sword to follow him. This handful of men, with only three field-pieces for their artillery, marched from Madras on the 26th of August, and on the 29th arrived at Conjeveram, a considerable town, with a large pagoda, lying about forty miles inland, where they received intelligence that the fort of Arcot was garrisoned by 1100 men; on which Captain Clive wrote word to Madras, desiring that two eighteen-pounders might be sent after him without any delay. On the 31st he halted within ten miles of Arcot, where the enemy's spies reported, that they had discovered the English marching with unconcern through a violent storm of thunder, lightning, and rain: and this circumstance, from their notions of omens, gave the garrison so high an opinion of the fortitude of the approaching enemy, that they instantly abandoned the fort, and a few hours after the English entered the city, which had no walls or defences, and marching through 100,000 spectators, who gazed on them with admiration and respect, took possession of the fort, in which they found a large quantity of lead and gunpowder, with eight pieces of cannon, from four to eight-pounders. The merchants had, for security, deposited in the fort effects to the value of 50,000l; but these were punctually restored to the owners; and this judicious abstemiousness conciliated many of the principal inhabitants to the English interest. The fort was inhabited by 3000 or 4000 persons, who, at their own request, were permitted to remain in their dwellings[157].*

William Hunter in his *Rulers of India: Lord Clive* also notes that Clive arrived and left Kanchipuram in the midst of a storm[158].

> *On the 29th the little force reached Kanchipuram, 42 miles from Madras and 27 from Arcot. There he learned that that place was garrisoned by about 1200 native soldiers, that the discipline was lax, and that a surprise was quite feasible; but that the place itself was capable of a good defence. He did not wait longer. Setting out in a terrible storm, he reached the vicinity of Arcot on the 31st...*

That Lord Varadaraja's grace was upon Clive could be construed (if looked upon from the angle of faith) by the following instance during the siege of Arcot:

---

157 Malcolm, Sir John (1836). Life of Robert, Lord Clive: Collected from the Family Papers communicated by the Earl of Powis, London: John Murray, para 73-74.

158 Hunter, William Wilson (1893). Rulers of India: Lord Clive, London: Oxford University Press, Chapter VI: The First Years of Soldiering at Trichinopoli and Arcot.

Captain Clive had a series of wonderful escapes, and indeed the men began to regard him with a sort of superstitious reverence, believing that he had a charmed life. One of his three remaining officers, seeing an enemy taking deliberate aim at him through a window, endeavoured to pull him aside. The native changed his aim, and the officer fell dead. On three other occasions sergeants, who accompanied him on his rounds, were shot dead by his side. Yet no ball touched him[159] (p.62).

Furious at the fall of Arcot, Chanda Sahib dispatched his son Raza Sahib with 4000 French and native troops from Trichy to lay siege to Arcot. The siege resulted in huge loss of lives to Raza Sahib and loss of the throne to Chanda Sahib. Robert Clive returned to Fort St George with a strong ally in Muhammed Ali Walajah as Nawab of Arcot, and a vast cache of treasure as tribute.

On his way back, Clive halted at Conjeevaram. True to his vow, Clive paid homage to Varadaraja, thanking him for the victory. He also presented a MAKARAKANDI, an invaluable emerald encrusted necklace obtained from the treasury of Arcot. Even today, the Makarakandi is worn by the Lord on special occasions.

Clive went on to defeat Siraj Ud Daulah and his French allies in the battle of Plassey six years later. A strong foundation for British Indian Empire was laid by this victory. He would also accrue vast wealth and title on account of his exploits in India.

Lord Varadaraja of Kanchipuram

---

159 Henty, GA (n.d.). With Clive in India or the Beginnings of an Empire, Chapter 7: The Siege of Arcot. See Project Gutenberg ebook at https://www.gutenberg.org/cache/epub/18833/pg18833-images.html#Ch7.

Lord Varadaraja with Clive's Makarakandi

Pic courtesy: https://kazhiyurvaradanblog.in/2015/06/24/robert-clive-at-kancheepuram-temple/

14
William Garrow: A Matter of Faith

The curious thing about history is, it just occurs.

Indian history especially appears to be one long chapter in the history of the world with as many probabilities and improbabilities; ponderable and imponderable; myths and realities, generously interwoven so as to defy an ordinary understanding. This is also one such story that may belie reason but then, it is a fact of history.

We happened to drive down to Bhavani, a town that sits on the confluence of two major rivers of South India, Cauvery and Bhavani. Right at the confluence of both these rivers is the Sangameswara Temple, literally meaning "Lord of the Confluence". My mother was born in this town, at a mere walking distance from this temple and my father joined school here. The story of their union in marriage is 60 years old, but as full of life as these two mighty rivers to the Tamil region!

So, we were in the temple. As is customary, we prayed to the Lord first and then proceeded to the mother's sanctum. She is called Vedanayaki, meaning 'the one who is the soul of Vedas or the one who presides over the Vedas'. After our prayers, as we proceeded with circumambulation of the inner sanctum, we saw a stone inscription. Frankly, there are so many inscriptions in every temple and they usually attract very little attention. We too were about to walk past when a name and date in the inscription caught our attention – William Garrow, 11-01-1804. The inscription said an honourable Mr. William Garrow the collector of Salem presented a palanquin to the goddess with his utmost reverances.

We wondered as to why an English collector would become as devoted to this Hindu goddess as to present a palanquin. Now, here is the story:

William Garrow (1776-1815) was Collector of Salem District from July 1802. Once he arrived at Bhavani and was resting in the travelers' bungalow.

This bungalow incidentally adjoins the temple and even today looks every bit colonial!! Sometime in the night, he suddenly felt awakened and saw a young girl in front of him who was beckoning him to exit his room. Startled but curious, William came out of his room. As he tried to follow this young girl, she disappeared into the temple adjoining the bungalow.

Even as he tried to follow her, William Garrow was shocked to find roof of the room that he just left crashing down. A shaken William Garrow could not even hazard to think of his fate had he stayed indoors. The collector's staff and escorts were equally puzzled and proceeded to arrange some alternate place for him to rest. But William Garrow was quite dazed and curious to find out about the girl who apparently saved his life. In the course of the excitement that followed this collapse of the roof, the reminder of the night passed. Early next morning, priests of the temple arrived for "ushat Kala pooja" (ritualistic rites in the early morning).

They were also taken aback by the occurrences of the night. When quizzed by the collector as to the girl, they were completely at a loss since the temple remains locked after the evening worship and no one can enter the locked sanctum. William Garrow however was emphatic that the girl who saved his life entered the temple and disappeared. He pleaded with the preists to have this verified.

Entry of a non-Hindu into the sanctum was against the temple codes. But, finding the Collector insistent, the priests agreed to make a hole in the outer wall of the temple facing the deity. They then asked him to see whether the girl who saved his life was inside. When William Garrow looked inside the sanctum through the hole, he saw Vedanayaki Thayar (goddess). He realized and swore that the girl who appeared before him in the night was indeed goddess Vedanayaki!

The town of Bhavani was in amazement upon hearing this and William Garrow became an ardent devotee of Goddess Vedanayaki. He presented an ivory palanquin for the mother on 11 January 1804 and continued to visit the temple in later years to seek Her blessings.

Notes on William Garrow

This story inscribed in the stone plaque inspired me to check on William Garrow. What I found makes me say what I said in the beginning: The curious thing about history is, it just occurs.

Edward Garrow (1751-1820) who joined the East India Company at the age of 18 as a junior writer in 1769, later served as Mayor of Madras in 1782. Edward Garrow married Sophia Dawson of England in Fort St George. He also had many Indian women as his begums [Please read William Dalrymple's White Mughals[160]. It was common among white men to keep many begums, in the style of Mughals in India]. William Garrow was born to a native woman and Edward Garrow. William also had a sister, Myra. Edward and Sophia also had a son, George. Sophia and George spent their life only in England whereas William followed his father and served East India Company with distinction.

William Garrow rose to be the Collector of Salem and later Coimbatore. He is distinguished as an able administrator. His name figures as the first Collector to have sent English shikaris (sports hunters) to Nilgiris in 1812, paving way for the English to habitat Ootacamund[161].

It is also interesting to note that while William's father made his fortunes in India, his uncle, Sir William Garrow (1760-1840), is credited to be one of the most brilliant barristers in English history. In fact, Sir William Garrow (the uncle) is credited to have formulated the Adversarial System of jurisprudence that many countries follow today[162]. In recent times, the BBC TV produced a series titled *Garrow's Law,* commemorating the uncle. A book on Sir William Garrow is touted "to enter the nation's consciousness for his 'gifts to the world' - as the originator of the modern-day presumption of innocence, the right to universal legal representation and access to justice in a criminal court, expert crossexamination and early traces of human rights"[163].

The Sangameswara temple is also a treat to art/culture lovers with exquisite sculptures that reflect the rich architectural traditions of Tamil Nadu.

Bhakthi as India teaches us, is not just about rituals and practices. It is about faith that transcends cultures.

---

160 Dalrymple, William. (2003). White Mughals: love and betrayal in eighteenth-century India. New York: Viking.

161 Vijaya Ramadas Mandala (Ed) (2019). Shooting a Tiger: Big-Game Hunting and Conservation in Colonial India, New Delhi: OUP.

162 John Hostettler and Richard Braby (2009), Sir William Garrow: His Life, Times and Fight for Justice, London: Waterside Press Ltd.

163 https://www.wildy.com/isbn/9781904380559/sir-william-garrow-his-life-times-and-fight-for-justice-hardback-waterside-press

The stone inscription commemorating William Garrow's present of a palanquin

The hole in the wall from which William Garrow saw the Goddess

Architechrual wonders of the temple:

Source: Photos by author.

15
Sir Thomas Munro and the Story of Mantralaya

Sir Thomas Munro was the Governor of Madras Province from 1820 to 1827. He is credited as the father of Ryotwari system in which taxes for agricultural land were directly collected from ryots (owners of individual plots of land) as contrasted to Zamindari system followed in Bengal in which Zamindars were given the task of collecting revenues.

Twenty years before becoming Governor of Madras Province, Munro (then a Major in the Company Army) served as Collector of Kurnool[164] that was ceded to East India Company by Tipu Sultan after his defeat in the First Anglo-Mysore war. Munro undertook detailed surveys of land in the area and fixed rents and taxes on a uniform scale. He discharged his duty with a commitment and sense of responsibility that went beyond the charter vested in him by East India Company, as seen from historical records:

> In 1802-3 the land suffered from draught and famine, and in the following years from excessive rains. In a report to the Board (at Madras), Munro calculated that 1,000 tanks and 800 channels had been breached in Cuddapah District, and he estimated the cost of repairs at seven lakhs of rupees. Without waiting for orders of Government, Munro ordered his subordinates to spend an almost unlimited amount, and the repairs were so speedily effected that, the following years being good, he was able to report that 'the settlement was nearly as high as it need be, and it is not likely that for some years it can receive any material augmentation[165]'.

In the process of delineating lands, he was unable to determine extent of

---
164 Govt of AP (1974). Kurnool District Gazette, p 54.
165 Bradshaw, John (1894). Rulers of India: Sir Thomas Munro and the British Settlement of the Madras Presidency, Oxford: The Clarendon Press, p 120.

lands that were controlled by the Mutt at Mantralaya, where Sri Raghavendra Swami's Samadhi is located. Under extant policy of East India Company, lands were to be directly taken over by the Company where ownership was not clear. Before doing so, Sir Munro made one more attempt and was told by the priests that only Sri Raghavendra Swami can provide clear answers since no one else seemed to know.

Sri Raghavendra Swami was a great saint who lived from 1595 to 1671 and attained Brahma Samadhi[166] at Mantralaya. He is considered to be a living saint and tradition says that Sri Raghavendra Swami would continue to live for 700 years[167] after his Brahma Samadhi[168]. Mantralayam continues to attract thousands of devotees. People worshiping him continue to report his miracles even today.

By the time Major Munro was told about the Swami, Sri Raghavendra had been in Samadhi for nearly 130 years. Sir Munro was therefore taken aback by the conviction of people who told him to meet Sri Raghavendra Swami for getting clarifications on land issues. Both curious as well as determined to complete his task, Munro decided to meet the Swami. On arriving at Mantralaya, Sir Munro removed his shoes and hat, washed, and sat in front of the Samadhi and prayed. To his great surprise and awe, Sri Raghavendra Swami appeared before him and patiently explained to him the extent of land belonging to the Mutt and the village. Sir Munro took notes, thanked the Swami and returned to his office.

Being the collector, he proceeded to make appropriate orders apportioning specified lands to the Mutt in revenue records. Munro's orders were later published in Madras Government Gazette in Chapter XI, page 213, 1820, the copies of which are available in State Government Archives at Chennai.

The story of Mantralaya is not to be viewed in isolation or as having been founded in myth. The English arrived in India without any understanding of its vastness, diversity and a highly evolved civilization. The tumultuous aftermath of collapse of the Moghul Empire afforded them an opportunity to ascend

---

166 The concept of Brahma Samadhi is peculiar to Hindu religion. While the scriptures describe it in detail through the schools of Dvaita, Advaita and Visishtadvaita, in simple terms it refers to a saint giving up his physical body and merging with the eternal super-consciousness at a time of his/her choosing.

167 Raghavendra Ashtothra Shatanamavali by Sri. Appanacharya of Bichali village that is across the Tungabadra River in Raichur District of Karnataka, from Mantralayam. He is a contemporary and disciple of Swamy Raghavendra.

168 The Raghavendra Charita refers to this.

to political power. However, politics is not the only dimension that defines subcontinental society. Commencing from kingdoms of yore that find detailed mention in the Ramayana, Mahabharata and various puranic recounts, India had a highly evolved political process. More importantly, the spiritual dimension that it attained stands on a platform of its own, sometimes intertwined with political process and at most others charting a path of its own.

When see from the life and belief of Sir Munro it is possible to apportion credibility to the story of Mantralaya, apart from the cited archival record regarding the land. Following is an extract from his correspondences from Darmavaram dated 30th December 1815 with his sister Lady Erskine, where he shares his views relevant to the subject above[169] (See image).

It is evident that he held the saints of India in very high regard noting that their abstinence is real and even though they travel in state, they amass no wealth. He also notes great princes and nobles going to them in obeisance and seek guidance. It is possible to possess such impressions only when one deeply appreciates the culture of the ruled as much as he esteems his own.

> SIR THOMAS MUNRO. 213
>
> priests of Pagodas, whom Europeans in general suppose to be at the head of the ecclesiastical establishment, are on the contrary an inferior class of Brahmins, who are regarded merely as servants of the Pagodas, and have no influence among the people; but the Swamis possess an influence not inferior to that of the Pope and his bishops and cardinals in the darkest ages. There are two principal ones, whose authority is acknowledged all over India; there are also several whose jurisdiction is limited to particular sects of Hindoos. The two principal have many subordinate Swamis, like cardinals and bishops, who in their respective districts settle all points of religion and cast. They have villages and sometimes whole districts allotted for their maintenance. All Hindoos treat not only the principal but their inferior Swamis with the highest respect; the greatest princes go out to meet them, and bow down before them. The Swamis do not marry like the Pagoda Brahmins, but must lead a life of celibacy and temperance, or rather abstinence. They have no nephews and nieces like the Swamis of Europe. Their abstinence is real, their diet is more simple than that of a peasant. They travel in state with elephants, palanquins, drums, and standards, but they amass no wealth. Whatever they receive they distribute as fast as they get it, and on the whole they are to the full as respectable as their brethren in Europe.

---

169 Gleig, GR (1830). Life of Sir Thomas Munro, London: Henry Colburn and Richard Bentley, p 212-213

Epilogue

I had mentioned in the introduction and the chapter on historical context that the purpose of this book is to interrogate history to ascertain the context for each of the stories. I was driven by two interests: one, to narrate the story and, two, to verify the occurrence through historical evidence. Only the readers can say whether this has been achieved.

All players in the described events are part of the living memory of South Indian society. Such living memories and oral narratives do mutate over many generations. As time passes, some of these players may attain characteristics that they never perhaps imagined they will. Societies have a tendency to view historical personages through the prism of their current experiences and opinions, in the process transforming their entire persona. But a researcher has a duty – the duty to construct events as permitted by available evidence.

When such a construction takes place, no claim can be laid as to its infallibility. For, history does use imagination as a glue to logically bind together what it finds. To the extent that this glue is unaffected by personal prejudice, a logical construction facilitates the most probable version of that event. Did I suffer from any such prejudice? I would not imagine any, except a desire to stand in judgment of what I discovered and strictly limiting it to that particular historical context.

I do have another wish - South India needs to be studied more. Its kingdoms, culture and way of life do have many factors common with that of its north. While these binding threads are important to foster and strengthen national life, the distinctiveness of southern culture including its sub-cultures, needs to be recognized. Each of the sub-cultures in south have their own stories dating back millennia. For example, scholars claim that the 1st Tamil Sangam existed some 4400 years[1] before Christ, a period that even precedes the age of the Vedas. Literary standards of 1st Tamil Sangam works like Perumparipadal, Mudukuruku, Mudunarai and Kalariyavirai show that the Tamil society was more advanced in its intellectual achievements than any of its contemporaries.

---

1   Daniélou, A. (2003). A Brief History of India, Kenneth F. Hurry (Tr.), United States: Inner Traditions/Bear.

It needs no argument to say that an advanced civilization originates from a stable society with deep roots in history. No additional argument is needed to say that such a society is endowed with a rich store house of oral narratives too.

It is unfortunate that the present system of education fosters no curiosity to discover so rich a past through its written and oral narratives. I for one, having attained some decent levels of formal education, feel utterly disadvantaged even to hazard a journey of discovering this rich cultural heritage. Reason for this quaking feeling is much simpler: credible sources are either locked away in ancient archives where retrieval is a major challenge or they simply do not exist. If only a larger and more accessible repository of archival material is available in each district and zone where students and researchers can access their physical content or even electronic renderings, discovery of the rich cultural and historical heritage would become most pleasant.

I do pray that in the years to come discovery of ancient knowledge will become a passion in India. Such a discovery, when blended with contemporary scholarship across the world, will result in Atmanirbartha that India is actively pursuing to achieve. For, only a leader in knowledge can lead the world.

Index

A

Abdullah 5, 9, 51, 55, 56, 59
Acharya 1, 40, 41
Advaita 21, 90
Agraharam xi
Ajayaraja 29, 30
Akademi 59
Akkanna 55, 56, 57, 58, 59, 61
Aladdin xxi, xxii
Alamelu 70
Alexander xxv, xxviii
Alipiri vii, 51, 53
Allauddin xxix, xxx, xxxii, xxxiii, xxxiv, 1, 5, 9, 14, 15, 33
Alvars 13
Andhra xxxi, xxxiii, 14, 55, 69, 70, 71
Anegundi xxxiv, 15, 46, 47
Apadana xxviii
Arabic xxi
Arjuna xi
Article xxii, xxiii
Asceticism 21
Ashraf xxxv
Aurangzeb xxx, 51, 56, 60, 61
Azhagiya xxvii, 2, 6, 10, 13, 15, 16

B

Baguli 29
Balaji 70, 71
Banarsi xxix, xxxii, xxxiii, 15
Barani xxxv, 14, 35
Basavappa 41
Battle xxix
Battuta 36
Bhakta 55, 59, 62, 64
Bhamani xxxiv, xxxv
Bhanuji 55
Bharathi 39, 40, 42
Bhattar 17
Bhavani 85, 86
Brahma xv, xix, 49, 90
Brahmastra xix
Brahmins 47, 55
Britannica xxii
British 40, 73, 79, 80, 82, 89

C

Capital 47
Carnatic 79
Catalogue 47
Century xxx, 56
Chanda 79, 80, 82
Charanam 65, 66
Charles xxii, 35, 36
Chatrapati xx
Cheluva 23, 24, 25, 28
Chennai 5, 9, 15, 21, 22, 25, 90
Chittoor 53, 71
Cholapuram xxx, 22
Collector 53, 85, 86, 87, 89
Commentary 49
Company 13, 39, 53, 79, 81, 87, 89, 90
Confluence 85
Congress xxix, xxxiii, 15
Convention xxii, xxiii
Copyright vi
Cotton 47
Cultural xv, xxii, 26
Culture xiii

D

Dalrymple 87
Dargah xiii
Darius xxviii
Dawson 28, 87

Deccan xx, xxx, 14, 47, 60, 61, 71
Devagiri xxxi, xxxii, xxxiii, 14, 36, 45, 61
Devuni 69, 71
Dharma xix
Dharwar 39
Digvijayam 22, 25, 26, 49
District 35, 53, 55, 73, 85, 89, 90
Divine 61
Duryodhan 76
Duryodhana vii, 73, 75, 76, 77

E

Eastern xxvii, xxxii
Edward 87
Elliot 14, 28, 35
Emperor xxvii, 51, 56, 73
Emperors 39
Empire vii, xx, xxi, xxx, xxxiv, 2, 13, 15, 28, 34, 37, 40, 45, 46, 47, 60, 61, 79, 82, 90
England 79, 87
English xvi, xxi, 22, 25, 39, 43, 79, 80, 81, 85, 87, 90
European 47
Evidence xvi

F

Festival 77
Following 40, 91
Foreign xxv
Francis 35
French xxi, 79, 82

G

Galland xxi, xxii
Garrow vii, 85, 86, 87
General 79
George 34, 35, 52, 80, 82, 87
Ghazna 29
Ghaznavi 27

Ghaznavid 27, 28, 29
Ghazni xxix, 27, 28
Ghurid 27
Ghurids 26, 27
Ghyasuddin 14
Goddess 37, 48, 70, 86
Golconda xxxiv, xxxv, 51, 52, 55, 56, 57, 58, 60, 61, 65
Gopanna 15, 16, 17, 18, 55, 57, 58, 59
Gopuram 3
Government 14, 28, 55, 56, 64, 89, 90
Governor 79, 89
Gujarat xxix, xxxii, 27
Gutenberg 82

H

Hanuman 61
Harihara xx, xxxiv, 15, 16, 39, 40, 45, 46, 47, 48, 49
Hazarat xiii, 56, 57
Heritage xxii, 26
Historians xiii, xxvii, xxx, xxxi, xxxiii, 14, 15, 26, 47
Historical i, iii, vii, xxiv, xxvii, 16, 26, 29, 48
History xiii, xx, xxii, xxiii, xxiv, xxix, xxx, xxxii, xxxiii, xxxiv, 14, 15, 22, 26, 28, 29, 34, 36, 45, 46, 47, 52, 53, 56, 60
Hospet 47
Hunter 81

I

Ibrahim 29, 59, 60
Ikshvaku 65, 66
Indian xi, xiii, xv, xvi, xviii, xix, xx, xxvii, xxviii, xxix, xxxi, xxxiii, 14, 15, 27, 28, 29, 45, 48, 49, 56, 60, 72, 73, 77, 80, 82, 85, 87
Indigenous xxiv
Invasions i, iii, xxviii, xxxii

Index

J

Jalaudin 36
Johnston 47
Journal xvi, 10, 46, 56
Justice 87

K

Kadapa 69, 71
Kakatiya xxxii, xxxiii, xxxiv, 1, 14, 15, 36, 45
Kākatiyas 14
Kalyani 23, 30
Kampili 36, 45, 46, 47
Kannan xiv
Karnatak 51, 52
Karnataka xiv, xxxi, 1, 15, 22, 90
Kerala xxviii, xxxii, 36, 56, 73, 74, 75, 76
Khaliq xxix, xxxiii, 15
Khalji xxix, xxxii, xxxiii, 15
Khaljis xxix, xxxii, xxxiii, 15
Khilji xxix, xxx, xxxii, xxxiii, xxxiv, 1, 5, 13, 14, 15, 33, 35
Kingdom xviii, 48
Kishore 29
Kodava 7, 9, 13, 15, 16
Kollam 73, 75, 76
Kootam xiv
Kotagiri 14
Krishna xxx, xxxi, 25, 30, 45
Kumara xiv, xxxiv, 15, 18, 36, 37
Kurava 75, 76
Kurnool 71, 72, 89

L

Lakshmana 66
Lakshmi 23, 69, 70, 71
Languages 47
Legend 75
Leiden 47, 48
Lennart 47, 48
Letter 43
Literary xxx, 47
London xxii, xxxii, 14, 28, 33, 36, 47, 74, 81, 87, 91
Looting vii, 33

M

Mackenzie 47
Madanna 55, 56, 57, 58, 59, 61, 62
Madhavam 49
Madras xv, 15, 22, 35, 52, 53, 61, 79, 80, 81, 87, 89, 90
Madurai vii, xxii, xxxii, xxxiii, xxxiv, xxxv, 1, 2, 5, 14, 18, 33, 34, 35, 36, 37, 46, 51
Mahabali 73, 74, 75
Mahapurna 21
Mahmud 27, 28
Malabar 1, 14, 35
Malakkuda 76
Malanada 76
Manavala xxvii, 2, 6, 10, 13, 15, 16
Mankachar 51
Mantralaya vii, 89, 90, 91
Maratha xx, 39, 40, 55
Mathura xxix, 28, 29, 30
Matsya xv
Meenakshi 34, 35, 37
Melukote xiv, 22, 23, 24, 25, 26, 28, 30
Ministers 56
Mohammed xxix, 14, 53
Mohammedan 1, 2, 5
Mongol xxxiii
Monograph 47
Mousavi xxviii
Mubharak xxxiv
Mughals xx, 15, 87
Muhammad xxviii, xxxiv, 13, 14, 15, 16, 27, 36, 37, 45, 52
Muhammadan xxxii, 14
Murthi 5
Murugan xiii, xiv, 31
Muslim xiii, xiv, xx, xxii, xxviii, xxix, xxxi, xxxiv, xxxv, 1, 2, 7, 9, 10, 11, 13, 16,

22, 26, 28, 30, 33, 34, 35, 36, 37, 45, 46, 52, 60, 70, 71
Mysore 25, 28, 30, 35, 39, 40, 41, 89

N

Nachiar vii, 9, 10, 13, 16, 21, 26, 30, 52, 70, 72
Namperumal vii, 13, 18
Narayana 22, 23, 26, 28
Narmada xxix, xxxi, xxxii, xxxiv, 7, 14, 28, 45
Native xxiv
Nayaks 51, 52
Nights xxi, xxii
Nilakanta xii, 34, 47
Nizami xxix, xxxiii, 15

O

Oxford xxxii, xxxiii, xxxiv, 21, 22, 34, 45, 81, 89

P

Palace xxviii, 73
Pallava xxxi
Pandava 69, 75
Pandya xxvii, xxx, xxxi, xxxii, xxxiii, 1, 2, 14, 15, 33, 34, 36, 46
Parabrahma 14
Parasurama 73
Periplus xxvii, xxviii
Persia xxviii, 51
Portuguese 73
Poruvazhy 76
Practice xxxiii
Pradesh xiii, xxxi, 14, 55, 69, 70, 71
Prakasa 21
Prasad xxix, xxxii, xxxiii, 15, 49
Priests 60
Prince xxx, 13, 14, 45, 46
Provinces 28

Publisher vi
Pulakesin xxxi
Pulicat 51, 52
Punjab 27
Purana xv, 69
Puranic 69
Pushkarani 23, 30

Q

Qutbuddin xxix

R

Raghunatha 55
Rajasthan xxix, 27, 29
Ramadasu vii, 55, 58, 59, 60, 61, 62, 64, 65, 66
Ramanuja vii, 21, 22, 23, 25, 26, 27, 28, 30, 72
Ramapriya 25, 30
Ramayana xviii, xix, xxv, 57, 58, 73, 91
Ranganatha ix, 1, 5, 6, 13, 17, 21
Ravuttar xiii, xiv
Records xxvii, 40, 42, 43
Rekapalli 59
Religious 58
Report 28
Richard xx, xxxv, 10, 14, 87, 91
Robert vii, xii, 13, 15, 45, 48, 79, 80, 81, 82

S

Sadarat 15
Sahitya 59
Samadhi 90
Sangama 15, 45
Sankara 49
Sastra xv
Sastry 14, 47
Sataka xx
Saunders 79, 80
School 21

Scriptures 21
Scroll xxxv
Service 72
Settlement 89
Shankara xx, 21, 40
Sharada 40, 41
Shastry 40, 42, 43
Shaybani 29
Shikoh xxx
Shilpa xv
Shivaji xx
Social xi, xx, xxiii, 14, 46, 47, 56, 60
Society xxxiii
Sophia 87
Sources 47
Sringeri vii, 39, 40, 41, 42, 43, 48, 49
Srinivasan iii, ix, xii, xv
Studies xvi, xxxv, 10
Sultan vii, 13, 27, 39, 40, 41, 43, 47, 55, 57, 58, 89
Sultanat xxix, xxxiii, 15
Sultanate xxix, xxxii, 1, 2, 5, 15, 26, 36, 46
Sundara xxxii, xxxiii, 1, 33, 34
Suradhani 6, 7, 9, 10, 72

T

Taghatigin 29
Tanjore xxxv, 9, 31, 51
Tarain xxix, 27
Tehsil 57
Tehsildar 57
Temple i, iii, vii, xxx, xxxv, 22, 24, 31, 37, 69, 70, 71, 73, 76, 85
Temples i, iii, xxxii
Thayar 1, 17, 18, 86
The Hindu xiv, 31, 70
Thodarntha vii, 5, 6, 7, 9, 13, 52, 72
Thomas vii, 73, 79, 89, 91
Thousand xxi
Tirupati xiv, 7, 9, 13, 15, 16, 22, 41, 52, 53, 69, 70, 72
Tradition xxii, xxiii, xxiv, 46, 69
Trichy xxvii, 79, 82

Tughlaq xxxiv, 13, 14, 15, 16, 36, 37, 45, 46, 52
Tukaram xx
Tulukka vii, 9, 10, 13, 16, 26, 30, 52, 70, 72

U

UNESCO xxii, xxx
University xvi, xix, xx, xxxii, xxxiii, xxxiv, 14, 21, 22, 28, 29, 34, 35, 36, 45, 47, 48, 56, 69, 81
Utsava 5

V

Vairagya xx
Vaishnavas 22
Valley xiii
Vamana xv, 73, 74
Varadaraja 21, 80, 81, 82, 83
Varaha xv, 52, 60, 65
Varanasi xxx, 29, 48
Vasishta xviii, xix
Vedanayaki 85, 86
Vellai 3
Vellayi vii, 1, 2, 3, 9, 16
Vellore xxxv, 51
Victory 47
Vidyaranya vii, xx, xxi, 39, 40, 45, 46, 47, 48, 49
Vishnu xv, 13, 22, 69, 73, 74, 80

W

Walajah 79, 80, 82
Warangal xxxii, xxxiii, xxxiv, 1, 5, 14, 15, 45, 46
William vii, 81, 85, 86, 87

Y

Yadava xxxi, xxxii, xxxiii, xxxiv, 14, 21, 36, 45

www.ingramcontent.com/pod-product-compliance
Ingram Content Group UK Ltd.
Pitfield, Milton Keynes, MK11 3LW, UK
UKHW022153230426
12049UKWH00003BA/85